Faith

HOLY BIBLE

Minister Mary D. Edwards

Use It...
or Lose It!

Minister Mary D. Edwards
with Foreword by The Rev. Dr. Stanley L. Scott

For more information, contact:
Minister Mary D. Edwards
Leaves of Gold Consulting, LLC
LeavesofGoldConsulting.com
Leavesofgold.llc@gmail.com

Book cover and page design by
Shannon Crowley for Treasure Image & Publishing

Dedication

*This book is dedicated in loving memory
to my mother,
Audrey Gertrude (Fountaine) Pennamon
May 29, 1924-January 25, 1996*

*During some of my most trying
times, I could see her lapel pen
that she loved to wear. It read:
"I'VE GOT FAITH!"*

Acknowledgements

From the bottom of my heart, I wish to thank the following for their commitment to this project.

Dr. Stanley L. Scott, my esteemed pastor, Salvation Temple church in Detroit. When I joined his church, he promised to be the best pastor I've ever had. My special name for him is *"Best Pastor."* That's how I address him. And I have no reluctance in doing so.

Mrs. Rosa Stephens, for her editorial suggestions. In spite of her very busy schedule, she stopped what she was doing when I came to her at the last minute for assistance.

Dr. Debby Mitchell, my dear friend and prayer partner for her review of the manuscript and valuable input.

Ms. Shannon Crowley for her creative work on the cover design and layout.

Minister Dorothy Butler for her encouragement and prayers.

Thanks to Pamela Osborne for her faithful friendship and professional support.

All of the writers who are fighting the good fight of faith and their willingness to share their very personal stories in this book.

-MDE-

Foreword

Hello Dear Reader,

This book that you are holding is more like a journey into a new realm of living in peace and confidence through FAITH that is "used" every step of the way!

Actually, I would really want to invite you to take your time going through this book. I believe that you will be best served by having a quiet place, get into a relaxed satisfying environment, and allow your heart to be open to the gentle touch of Holy Spirit as you absorb the wisdom from its pages.

My dear friend, Mary Edwards, has put together a masterful presentation on the concept of keeping FAITH alive, active and flourishing! FAITH: Use It or Lose It.

Mary's life and heart are in these pages. This work is practical and embraceable, because she is. She, and the other contributors to this assignment, earnestly reach out to you with messages that bring the big super spiritual ideals about FAITH into a place where FAITH can be readily understood and applied with confidence that produces victory.

I highly recommend this book to you in the hope that the calling of God on the life of Minister Mary Edwards will bring FAITH FILLED LIFE into clearer focus in you!

I am honored by God's grace to be her "Best Pastor".

Enjoy your journey.

God Bless,
The Rev. Dr. Stanley L. Scott
www.salvation-temple-church.org
888.898.WORD (9673)

Introduction

Were you to ask those who know me, they would tell you that I have great faith. Indeed, God has blessed me to receive recognition over the past 30 years for my work throughout Michigan and beyond. I've received awards from the city, county, state, governor and even the President of The United States of America. Churches, civic groups, and businesses also have honored me. To God be all the glory!

What many don't know is that there was a time I felt like throwing in the towel, facecloth AND the soap. I have had what can be described as many *"anticipointments."* My hopes were sky high and I was on cloud nine. Suddenly, it was as though the rug had been pulled out from under me. Health and financial issues had me on an emotional roller coaster: Up one day and down the next. My hope had come to a halt. My faith was spiraling downward and was about to hit rock bottom. I asked the Lord on a regular basis to send the rapture and get me out of here. I'm so glad that He didn't listen. Instead, He increased my faith. I'm still looking for the rapture, but I'm not homesick

What I'm about to share with you are the lessons I learned during this *"dry spell."* While we all have desert experiences from time to time, God wants us to learn *"desert etiquette."*

Let me leave this word with you:

NO RAIN, NO RAINBOW!

NO TEST. NO TESTIMONY!

Minister Mary Edwards
2009

Table of Contents

Part One

WHAT IS FAITH?

If you feel that someone is out to get you, you may not be paranoid. Your intuition may be revealing a truth to you.

The Bible tells us in St. John 10:10 that the thief comes to steal, kill and destroy God's people. Who is the *"thief?"* Biblically speaking, he is the Devil. Whether you want to admit it or not, there is a devil. The Bible calls him Lucifer and Satan. Whatever his name is, he is your enemy. And, indeed, he wants to steal your faith, your dreams, and eventually your soul. Let's begin this discourse with a brief definition of faith.

Faith can be described as *"confidence or trust in a person or thing: faith in another's ability; belief not based on proof."*

The Christian faith, which is what I will be emphasizing in this book, has existed since the time that Jesus Christ was on earth. Followers of Jesus have had different understandings about many things, but all true Christians agree that Jesus Christ is a revelation of God in the flesh. We all believe that, after the fall of Adam and Eve in the Garden of Eden, God came to earth to bring us back into a relationship with Himself. In order to be a Christian, we must accept all of this by *"faith,"* meaning we believe this without physical proof.

WHY HAVE FAITH IN GOD?

To have a relationship with God, we must first believe that He exists and that He hears and will answer our prayers.

We are commanded in Hebrews 11:23 to *"Have faith in God."* Since we are commanded to have faith in God, if we don't, we are disobedient and rebellious.

"Without faith it is impossible to please Him" (Hebrews 11:6). When we don't have faith, we don't please God.

Without faith in God we cannot be saved (born again). Without faith we cannot pray acceptably. And without faith we cannot live victoriously.

LEVELS OF FAITH

Do some people have more faith than others? Let's do some honest self-evaluation. Where do you see yourself?

> *"God hath dealt to every man a measure of faith"* **(Romans 12:3).**

That's enough to be saved. Hopefully, you don't stop there.

> *"O thou of little faith, wherefore didst thou doubt?"* **(Matthew 14:31).**

How often have you prayed,

"Lord, I believe. Help thou my unbelief"
(Mark 9:24).

*"And being not weak in faith, he considered
not his own body now dead, when he was
about 100 years old, neither yet the deadness of
Sarah's womb"* **(Romans 4:19).**

Father Abraham believed God because he disregarded his own frailties. Over and over again, Abraham passed the *"faith test."* God was impressed with Abraham's faith.

*"If it be so, our God whom we serve is able to
deliver us from the burning fiery furnace, and he
will deliver us out of thine hand, O king"*
(Daniel 3:17).

I call this *"fire-proof"* faith. When we are in our fiery trials, do we allow fear or faith to reign in our hearts?

*"Hearken, my beloved brethren, Hath not God
chosen the poor of this world rich in faith and
heirs of the kingdom which he hath promised to
them that love him?"* **(James 2:5,22).**

Rich faith should be our ultimate goal.

HOW DO WE OBTAIN, MAINTAIN AND INCREASE OUR FAITH?

Learn the word of God. The Bible says that, *"Faith cometh by hearing and hearing by the word of God"* (Romans 10:17).

Read the Bible! There you will find the promises of God.

Underline these promises, memorize the Scriptures, and quote them throughout the day.

Purchase a book with just the promises of God. Place it where you can find it in a hurry when you need an injection of faith. Listen to God's word on recordings. This will build your faith.

Take notes at all services in church.

Surround yourself with *"faith talking"* people.

Watch your words! Don't talk doubt when you need to be speaking faith.

Pray with a surrendered heart. Be willing to accept God's will – no matter what! God never gives faith for things contrary to His will.

Act on your faith. *"But wilt thou know, O vain man, that faith without works is dead?"* (James 2:20). One way to grow a great faith is to act on God's promises. Put God to the test. He will prove Himself and you will have a stronger assurance than ever before that you can rely on God's faithfulness.

Faith comes by asking for it. One of my favorite Scriptures is, *"Lord I believe; help thou my unbelief"* (Mark 9:24). Once you ask Him for something, start praising Him 24/7 before the prayer is answered. Remember, *"The joy of the Lord is your strength"* (Nehemiah 8:10).

"FAITH KILLERS"

Since the beginning of time, there has been spiritual warfare going on between good and evil, God and Satan. Here are some of Satan's strategies to destroy your faith. I call these *"Faith Killers."*

1. Distractions

The adversary deals with us through our five senses: see, hear, taste, touch, and smell. Satan wants to distract us by getting us to focus our attention (our eyes) on material things instead of the spiritual things of life, on men rather than God.

Keep your eyes on Him. Focus. Focus. Focus. Let me share with you a personal story. I call it *"Whatcha Looking At?"*

My cordless phone rang. By the time I found it, it had stopped and the answering machine had picked up. The familiar voice said, *"Mary, call me. I need to talk with you."* I love the person dearly, but she was always in distress, so I really preferred not to return the call. I was having a pretty good day and wanted it to stay that way. However, because I am not a fair-weather friend, I dialed her phone number.

As soon as I heard the tone of her voice, I wanted to hang up. But I knew she could see my name on the Caller ID, so I took a deep breath and said, *"Hey, Girl. You sound down. What's up?"*

Before I could get the words out of my mouth, she gave me a litany of complaints. I listened sympathetically for a while, but soon realized that this conversation could go on for hours.

I had a choice. I could start complaining about my own challenges, or I could turn the situation around. I decided to give my friend an illustration.

"I want you to close your eyes," I said. *"Now, envision a plain white sheet of paper. There is nothing on the paper, except for a small black dot in the center of the sheet. Tell me what do you see?"*

"A black dot," she replied.

"That's the problem," I told my friend. *"You are looking at the sheet of paper the same way you are looking at your life. Instead of seeing all of the white space, you are focusing on the black dot. Change your focus. Rather than staring at your problems, look at your blessings."*

When I heard her shout, *"Hallelujah. Thank You, Jesus,"* I knew I had made a breakthrough.

And I was awfully glad that I had answered that call.

We're talking about distractions. Are you seeing spots? If so, it's time to clear your focus.

Samson is a good example of someone who let the wrong thing get into his eye gate (Delilah). You will find Judges, chapter 16, some very interesting reading. Start with verse one:

"Then went Samson to Gaza, and saw there an harlot, and went in onto her."

And then there's King David and Bathsheba. We all know that story. If not, check it out:

"And it came to pass in an eveningtide, that David arose from off his bed, and walked upon the roof of the king's house: and from the roof he saw a woman washing herself; and the woman was very beautiful to look upon" **(2 Samuel 11).**

Now, let me talk to you for a moment about a mirage. This definition is taken from the Webster Dictionary. Although it's long, there is a lot of substance in it – even spiritual insight.

A mirage is a special effect that is sometimes seen at sea, in the desert, or over a hot pavement, that may have the appearance of a pool of water or a mirror in which distant objects are seen inverted, and that is caused by the bending or reflection of rays of light by a layer of heated air of varying density, something illusory and unattainable like a mirage; a delusion; an optical illusion. A mirage is not a scent. It is not a sound. It is a sight. Something that is seen with the eye.

I repeat, seen with the eye. Are you in the midst of a spiritual storm (sea)? Then see it as just a mirage, and just a distraction. Perhaps you are in a dry place (desert). Or going through the fire (hot pavement). What do you see? What kind of eyes are you looking through? Natural or spiritual eyes?

In Webster's definition of mirage is the word *"inverted."* Inverted means: *"Something turned inside out or upside down. To reverse positions."* Are you getting the message? A mirage lends credence to the adage, *"Don't believe everything you hear and only half of what you see."*

Oftentimes when we go through life's trials and tribulations, we begin to see things that are not really there. Our vision becomes blurred and we have optical illusions. Things are not really as dreadful as they appear. But if we allow ourselves to be deceived, to have optical illusions, fear will set in. One popular Bible teacher, Joyce Meyer, says *"Fear is false evidence appearing real"* (_F_alse _E_vidence _A_ppearing _R_eal).

Recently, I noticed that the side view mirror on my car had the warning, *"Objects appear closer than they are."* Now this is a good optical illusion. One that should be taken seriously for safety sake. However, when our eyes start *"playing tricks on us,"* we need to be careful to consider the source and the motive, and become vigilant about choosing faith not fear

Thus, when we are going through a hard place, we cannot trust what we see with our natural eyes, which are made of flesh. But we must seek God for spiritual vision. What we see with natural eyes is temporary and of this world. What we see with spiritual eyes is eternal and of God.

Finally, friend, God will always provide a way to escape when we find ourselves between a rock and a hard place. But be very sure that the Rock is Jesus. He can be likened unto an *"oasis."* An oasis, which is found in the desert, is *"a fertile or green area in an arid region. Something providing relief from boring or dreary routine, a refuge."* Jesus is our Refuge. (Psalm 46:1-5).

Another point of entry for the adversary is the ear gate. It's not true when they say, *"Sticks and stones will break my bones, but names will never hurt me."* There is life and death in the power of the tongue and what people say to us can have tremendous impact on our self-esteem, whether negative or positive. Physical wounds heal a lot faster than emotional ones. Cruel words can steal our faith. Kind words can build it up.

Also, the ear gate is a very powerful doorway into our hearts and minds. The ear gate is responsible for no less than half and maybe much more of what we receive from the Word of God.

What are we listening to? Seriously consider what we are listening to from the television, radio, and those around us. We must have *"selective hearing."* God doesn't want us to voluntarily expose ourselves to the negative sounds and voices around us. Then there is the eye gate. The eye gate must be directed like a radar antenna. The eye gate cannot read a book laying directly on the table behind us. But our ear gate can record a message from behind us. Remember: garbage in, garbage out. We need to trash the trash. The following story is taken from my book, *Ponderings From the Heart of Mary.*

Trash the Trash

"When are you going to stop and pick up that debris?"' The Voice said to me. *"Who, me?"* I asked.

"Don't play dumb with me," said the quiet and gentle Voice. *"Don't be ignorant. You know Who this is speaking to you,"* the Voice continued. Conviction fell upon me. The Holy Spirit was trying to get my attention.

All week long, as I hurried into the house after a long and challenging day, I had procrastinated about picking up the trash that was accumulating on my front lawn. At first it was just one potato chip bag. The next day it was a candy wrapper peeking out at me from between the shrubs. Where did all of this trash come from? It had blown onto my lawn from one of my lazy or procrastinating neighbors who had done the same thing that I was now doing – ignoring the debris.

Our bodies are the temples of the Holy Spirit. We are to be good stewards over them. The trash we allow to go into our ears unchecked can grow rapidly and begin to contaminate us and the lives of those around us, much like the trash mentioned earlier. It spreads like wildfire. It can cause the property values of our spiritual houses to decrease.

So, I asked myself: *"Why am I sitting here writing this when I need to be outside removing the debris from my front lawn?"* The answer is simple but insufficient: We do those things that we enjoy doing and those that we don't enjoy become low priority items – until we find ourselves buried in debris. So we must be persistent about keeping God's word in our ears and before our eyes.

Now, back to what we allow to enter our senses. Taste can lead us into temptation, if we get an appetite for the wrong things.

Just look around. Our obesity rate is enormous. What are you putting in your mouth?

Aromatherapy oils can be very healing as they drift throughout our nostrils and we smell that soothing fragrance. However, allowing marijuana to drift through our nostrils can be damaging to our bodies.

Touching the wrong thing can get us into a lot of trouble, such as harmlessly viewing a pornography magazine at your corner drugstore. Or getting too friendly with a co-worker of the opposite sex and you are married. Everything in life is not soft and cuddly. Keep in mind that roses have thorns.

Satan wants us to major on the minors and to minimize the majors. How important will what you are focusing on now be in the next five years? When our priorities are out of order, we become distracted. Evaluate your priorities. Rearrange when necessary: God, family, career. Do this prayerfully. This may not be easy to do. God gives wisdom and strength for the asking, and He is a God of order.

2. Discouragement

One of Satan's big guns is discouragement so that we will give up. Discouragement is a lack of hope. He wants us to believe that things are getting worse instead of better. Watch the national news and you will be convinced!

Sometimes people discourage us with their constant criticism. We get the feeling that we can't do anything right. What's the use of trying? Who are you? Know who you are. Love Thyself. Do some self-examination. Other people's negative opinion of you is their problem, not yours.

Never Too Old To Learn

By William Kuykendall

"By humility and the fear of the Lord are riches, and honour, and life."
(Proverbs 22:4)

(The following story was written by an 81-year old Sunday school teacher.)

As a church Sunday school teacher, a new chapter came into my life. An issue of evaluation became a part of my lesson plan.

One Sunday I was dutifully teaching my adult class when members of another adult class seated themselves in my classroom. I continued the discussion of the lesson until a visitor openly expressed a negative comment about my teaching method. I was hurt and faith in my ability to teach was shattered. The negative message led to my writing a letter of resignation to the Sunday school administrator.

Later, I received a call from the administrator responding to my resignation. I was asked to consider the spiritual welfare of the students. He offered suggestions for improving my teaching methodology and expressed his interest in my growing as a teacher.

I accepted his advice. Within weeks, my class enrollment grew, and my confidence as a teacher has been renewed. I am so glad that I came to realize that it is not about me. It's all about Him!

> *Kuykendall has claimed Detroit, Michigan as home, although his migration from San Antonio, Texas bears memories. Upon his graduation from Central State University, he pursued a career in library science. It is his love for literature and participation with The Called and Ready Writers that credits his creative skills.*
>
> *Email: willkuyken@aol.com*

Comparing ourselves to others also can lead to discouragement. We always fall short. Low self-esteem causes us to doubt God and ourselves.

Sometimes circumstances discourage us. God wants us on top of circumstances, not under them. Start climbing. Don't stumble over things behind you. Turn your stumbling blocks into stepping-stones.

There comes a time to make up our minds that, God helping us, we shall not be moved by the things happening around us; like the old spiritual says:

> *I shall not be, I shall not be moved,*
> *I shall not be, I shall not be moved,*
> *Just like a tree planted by the water, Lord,*
> *I shall not be moved.*

If anyone ever had a valid reason to be discouraged, it was King David. In I Samuel 30, we read that David had lost everything, His army was weighed down with grief and he was facing death from those he thought were his friends. But, one thing that David didn't do in the midst of his many challenges, was lose his faith in God. This was documented throughout the book of Psalms. David did not allow his mind to be envisioned by defeat. Likewise, we must not allow ourselves to focus on the negative aspects of life. And there will be many. If we do, we will be tempted to do one of two things: fight against the enemy in our own strength or flee the scene.

God wants us to be good soldiers and fight the good fight of faith. (1Timothy 6:12). Press into Him in prayer. Worry, doubt, and fear all lead to one thing – sin. Let us do as King David did:

1) He did not allow fear to overwhelm him.
2) He ignored threats from those around him.
3) He quickly turned to the Lord in prayer.
4) He acted on his faith and did what God told him to do.
5) Finally, David encouraged himself in the Lord. (I Samuel 30:4).

Discouragement is faith in the Devil.

BIG GOD! little devil

Faith: Use it or Lose It!

"You are of God, little children, and have overcome them: because greater is he that is in you, than he that is in the world" **(I John 4:4).**

Do you have big expectations that seem to be falling through the cracks? Don't be discouraged. God has big things in store for you. But, for these things to happen, there's something you must do.

YOU MUST SPEAK TO YOUR MOUNTAIN.

What is the mountain in your life? In these hard economic times, it may be a mountain of debt. Perhaps you have lost a job, a house, a car, or something else that was important to you. Maybe it is a loved one and you are experiencing a mountain of grief. Is it a broken relationship and your mountain is loneliness? Are you suffering from a long-term, life-threatening illness and your mountain is fear? Did a friend let you down and you are feeling a mountain of betrayal?

Whatever your setback or disappointment is, we are told to be of good cheer, (John 16:33). I want you to make a determination to laugh at least five times per day. Even if you don't feel like it. I've tried it and it works. What happened to me when I did it was this: I didn't feel like laughing at first, but then I found myself laughing just because I was laughing! It's contagious.

How big is your God? Mine is omnipotent, omniscient, and omnipresent. In other words, He is all-powerful, all knowing, and in all places. Speak to your mountain by daily <u>reading</u> and <u>quoting</u> some of these Scriptures:

> **<u>Ephesians 3:20</u>**, *"Now unto him that is able to do exceeding abundantly above all that we ask or think, according to the power that worketh in us."*

> **<u>Mark 10:27</u>**, *"And Jesus looking upon them saith, With men it is impossible, but not with God: for with God all things are possible."*

> **<u>Mark 11:14</u>**, *"Therefore I say unto you, What things soever ye desire, when ye pray, believe that ye receive them, and ye shall have them."*

> **<u>Acts 20:32</u>**, *"And now, brethren, I commend you to God, and to the word of his grace, which is able to build you up, and to give you an inheritance among all them which are sanctified."*

> **<u>2 Chronicles 20:15</u>**, *"And he said, Hearken ye, all Judah, and ye inhabitants of Jerusalem, and thou king Jehoshaphat, Thus saith the LORD unto you, Be not afraid nor dismayed by reason of this great multitude; for the battle is not yours, but God's."*

Remember, whatever you focus on the longest becomes the strongest. So shout now: **BIG GOD! little devil.** And watch that mountain turn into a molehill! Then tread upon that molehill!

TAKE THE MOUNTAIN!

"...so here I am today, eighty-five years old! I am still as strong today as the day that Moses sent me out; I am just as vigorous to go out to battle now as I was then. Now give

me this hill country that the Lord promised me that day" (Joshua 14:10b-12).

Remember, BIG GOD! *little devil.*

As we grow older, we may tend to feel like we are losing some of our vim and vigor. Perhaps you feel like your *"get up and go has got up and went."* You may need to step aside for a while and rest. Take a sabbatical. But once the Holy Spirit has refreshed you, get back on track. Get back on the path. Keep your eyes on the prize - the prize of the high calling of Jesus Christ. There's a job to be done: one that has been assigned to you, and no one can do it like you can. *"Therefore, the prisoner of the Lord, beseech you that ye walk worthy of the vocation wherewith ye are called"* (Ephesians 4:1).

Lord Prop Us Up...

Sometimes when I pray, I think of the old deacon who always prayed, *"Lord, prop us up on our leanin' side."* After hearing him pray that prayer many times, someone asked him why he prayed that prayer so fervently.

He answered, *"Well sir, you see, it's like this... I got an old barn out back. It's been there a long time; it's withstood a lot of weather; it's gone through a lot of storms, and it's stood for many years.*

It's still standing. But one day I noticed it was leaning to one side a bit. So I went and got some pine poles and propped it up on its leaning side so it wouldn't fall.

Then I got to thinking about that and how much I was like that old barn. I've been around a long time. I've withstood a lot of life's storms. I've withstood a lot of bad weather in life, I've withstood a lot of hard times, and I'm still standing. But I find myself leaning to one side from time to time, so I like to ask the Lord to prop us up on our leaning side, 'cause I figure a lot of us get to leaning at times.

Sometimes we get to leaning toward anger, leaning toward bitterness, leaning toward hatred, leaning toward cussing, leaning toward fear, leaning toward a lot of things that we shouldn't. So we need to pray, 'Lord, prop us up on our leaning side,' so we will stand straight and tall again, to glorify the Lord."

Author unknown

3. Disillusionment / Disappointment

Disillusionment is the state of being disenchanted or disappointed by unfulfilled expectations. This has been called *"anticipointment,"* when our eager anticipation turns into heavy disappointment. Proverbs 13:12 says, *"Hope deferred makes the heart sick; but when the desire cometh, it is a tree of life."*

The African American writer, Langston Hughes, expressed it this way:

What Happens to a Dream Deferred?
By Langston Hughes

Does it dry up
Like a raisin in the sun
Or fester like a sore
And then rot?
Does it stink like rotten meat
Or crust and sugar over
Like a syrupy sweet?
Maybe it just sags
Like a heavy load
Or does it explode?

We can become disillusioned when we expect people to be perfect. That's why we are exhorted by the Apostle Paul *"Be ye followers of me, even as I also am of Christ"* (I Corinthians 4:16). The Bible clearly says, *"There is none righteous. No not one"* (Romans 3:10).

When we truly seek God's will, rather than our own, we will not be disappointed because we know that He is working out all things for our good, according to His promise in Romans 8:28. All of us have had at least one shattered dream in our lifetime. This is not the time to give up. When God closes one door, He opens another one. We must keep on going, in spite of circumstances.

Mary, the mother of Jesus, is one of my heroines. Although she was blessed by God to be a chosen vessel, the mother of Jesus Christ, she had a cross to bear when Jesus chose to go to the cross. Her son's choice caused her to suffer.

Sometimes other people's choices cause us to likewise suffer. Do you have a daughter who had an abortion, or a son on drugs? The dream of a beautiful marriage that ended in divorce? A husband addicted to online pornography? The death of a loved one? A child born with a disability? Are you in a mid-life crisis? Any one of these disappointments can cause us great despair and to eventually lose our faith. You may feel like throwing in the towel, the facecloth AND the soap. Don't do it! Just as Jesus rose from the dead, He can resurrect your hopes, dreams, and revive your faith. He can make disillusionment and disappointment flee. Let Him do it!

4. Discontentment

In the Bible, the children of Israel wanted a king because the other nations had one. God did not want them to have a king. But they insisted. The Lord warned them that having a king would be to their disadvantage. (I Samuel 8:10). They insisted. God complied with their request and, just as He said, they lost what they had. The grass always looks greener on the other side. That is until you cross over the fence. We always must ask God what is His will for our lives? God has a plan for our lives. *"I know the plans I have for you, declares the Lord plans to prosper you and not to harm you, plans to give you hope and a future"* (Jeremiah 29:11 NIV).

Often times we are unhappy because we want things that make others unhappy. Figure that! Single women want to be married and married women want to be single.

Nine requisites for contented living by Johann Wolfgang von Goethe (1749-1832): (1) Health enough to make work a pleasure; (2) Wealth enough to support your needs; (3) Strength to battle difficulties and overcome them; (4) Grace enough to confess your sins and forsake them; (5) Patience enough to toil until some good is accomplished; (6) Charity enough to see some good in your neighbor; (7) Love enough to move you to be useful and helpful to others; (8) Faith enough to make real the things of God; (9) Hope enough to remove all anxious fears concerning the future.

5. Discord (division)

Satan's job is to divide and conquer. Too often, he is successful. He does this in the home, in the church, in the community, and on the job.

You have heard it said that, *"A house divided against itself cannot stand"* (Mark 3:25). When everyone wants to have their own way, trouble is bound to set in. We are told to esteem others above ourselves. (Philippians. 2:3). When we don't, a selfish spirit, which comes from Satan, gets in and brings discord into the home. There is a lot of truth to the saying, *"A family that prays together stays together."*

We can see this same selfishness in the church, community, and on our jobs. A lack of mutual respect leads to discord. Keep in mind that's exactly what Satan wants to happen. His M.O. (modus operandi) is to keep up confusion so that he can divide and conquer. His job is to bring discord. If we give him a toehold, he will get a foothold, and before we know it, he will have his whole ugly spirit in the midst of you, your family, church, and your job. He wants to keep us ignorant of his devices.

6. Disassociation

Fellowship is critical to keep our faith alive. Satan loves it when we separate ourselves from one another. We also are told in Hebrews 10:25 not to forget to assemble ourselves with other believers. Satan knows that there is strength in numbers. *"A three-fold cord is not easily broken"* (Ecclesiastes 4:12b).

Indeed, we all need a support group. In Exodus 17:12, we see that when Moses became tired from fighting the enemy, he sat down on a rock and his brother Aaron and his friend Hur each held up his arms so he could continue the fight against the Amalikites. Likewise, we need to surround ourselves with a support team. Remember, teamwork makes the dream work.

"Churchgoers are like coals in a fire. When they cling together they keep the flame aglow; when they separate, they die out." **Billy Graham, evangelist. Men of Integrity, Vol. 1, no. 1**

7. Disobedience

Disobedience can certainly cause us to lose our blessing. I encourage you to read Deuteronomy 11:26-28 and also the entire 28th chapter of Deuteronomy. Just as there are rewards for obedience, there are severe consequences for disobedience. We have a choice.

The Bible is full of honorable as well as dishonorable men and women. Some were obedient as well as disobedient. But I don't have to go that far back. While in the process of writing my personal history, there were many unpleasant things I had to record. Some of them relate to the women in my own family – me included. Some of the details caused me to fall on my face and repent for my ancestors, as well as myself. I was pretty discouraged until the Holy Spirit brought to my attention that there were four notorious women in the official family tree of Jesus (Matthew 1:1-16): Tamar, Rahab, Ruth, and Bathsheba.

Tamar seduced her father-in-law to get pregnant.

Rahab was a prostitute.

Ruth wasn't even Jewish and broke the law by marrying a Jewish man.

Bathsheba committed adultery with David, which resulted in her husband's murder.

The first recorded disobedience by a woman was in Genesis when Eve listened to the serpent instead of to God. As a result, sin entered the world.

Then we have Delilah who deceived Samson, cut off his hair, causing him to lose his strength.

Jezebel was full of pride and control.

Were they *"bad to the bone," "bad for a season, but not forever,"* or just *"bad for a moment?"* I believe we can all relate to at least one of them. I highly recommend Liz Curtis Higgs' book, <u>Bad Girls in the Bible</u>, if you desire to study this topic more clearly.

In addition to King David and Solomon, there were other disobedient men in the Bible as well. Even Abraham got impatient and laid with Hagar for the son that God promised would come from Sarah's womb. (Genesis 16). Another excellent example of man's disobedience is Jonah (Jonah 1:1).

Jonah is the reluctant biblical prophet whose story appears in the book named for him. God instructed Jonah to go east from Israel to Assyria to *"cry out"* against wickedness in the city of Nineveh.

Jonah flees in the opposite direction, by sea. A storm hits, the ship's sailors attribute it to Jonah's flight from God, and he volunteers to be thrown overboard. A fish swallows him and spews him out on land three days later. This time Jonah obeys God and goes to Nineveh, where his shouted warnings work: the people repent, and the mind of God, who would have punished the city, is changed. The story ends with Jonah arguing with God about why Nineveh was spared. Sometimes we obey God but still murmur on the inside. Beware!

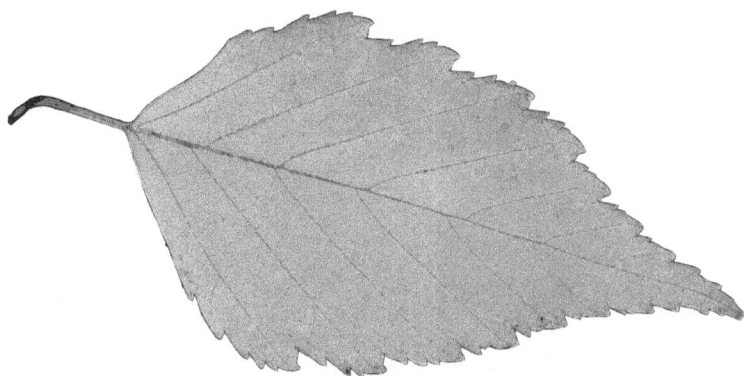

Part Two

Faith: Use it or Lose It!

WEARINESS

Weariness can open the door to many negative emotions such as anger, loneliness, self-pity, and confusion. All of these can lead to a loss of one's faith.

Sometimes people will plunge into a project and then the newness wears off. They get bored with it. Question: *"Did GOD assign this project to you? Did you pray about starting it? Is this just a good idea, rather than a God idea?"*

It's not unusual for people to just get tired of going to services, studying, resisting temptation, giving, and then they QUIT. I believe that one of the factors is a lack of balance. Man is a triune being, meaning we are a spirit, we have a soul, and we live in a body. Are you letting *"church"* overwhelm you? As the saying goes, *"Are you so spiritual minded that you are no earthly good?"* Do people enjoy being in your presence? Do you enjoy you?

We are told in 2 Thessalonians. 3:13 not to be weary. Yes. We can get tired, but we should not let it linger before getting refreshed. Even Jesus got tired from His journey and we see Him stopping at the well to get refreshed. (St. John 4:12) Throughout Scripture, we see Him going away to a solitary place and getting strengthened by His Father. We must do likewise.

One of my ministries is overseeing a support group for widows. I must admit that there are times when I find my energy drained. A lot of this comes from listening to their many challenges and helping them deal with their grief. Some of these widows haven't reached the level of spiritual maturity that I've been blessed to achieve. That's when I'm reminded of Jesus telling Peter to "*Feed my sheep,*" but He gave Peter nothing to feed them with. (St. John 21:17). In times like these, we become broken bread and poured-out wine. In other words, we are their nourishment until they learn how to feed on God. Please be careful to replenish your own soul less you become spiritually and physically exhausted. If you see yourself becoming a necessity in someone's life, know that you are out of God's will. We are servants to the "*Bridegroom.*" We must constantly be aware that our purpose is to point these people to Jesus. We must decrease so that He (God) can increase. (John 3:30).

To put it simply, "*GET OUT OF THE WAY!*"

To avoid weariness, we must rest our bodies. Do you prepare for bed? Or, at the end of the day, do you just jump in bed and pull the covers over your head? I hope not. You need to prepare for bed. Try taking a warm bath with soothing easy listening music, preferably instrumental. Light some candles. Aromatherapy works wonders. Ladies, add some bubble bath. Some of us, men and women, wait until the end of the day to get our exercise. Be careful. That can rev you up and keep you awake. Here's some good advice to both men and women: Just before getting into bed, turn off the television and say a prayer. *"God gives sweet sleep to His beloved"* (Proverbs 3:24).

Rest your mind. Many of our minds are on computer overload and headed for a crash. Thoughts are racing through our heads. Contrary to what it may seem, we cannot have more than one thought at a time in the same space in our head. Think about that! We must make a choice as to which thought we want to have at any given time. How nice it would be if we could just click off the switch before we are saturated with negative thinking. God wants us to have peace of mind, not a piece of mind. He gets no glory when our minds come to pieces. We must bring every thought into captivity to the obedience of Christ (2 Corinthians 10:5). Slow down, focus on Christ, and watch weariness flee!

IT'S ALL ABOUT ATTITUDE

Our attitudes are one of our most important assets.

In his book, *Improving Your Serve*, Chuck Swindoll said, *"The longer I live, the more I realize the impact of attitude on life. Attitude, to me, is more important than facts. It is more important than the past, than education, than money, than circumstances, than failures, than successes, than what other people think or say or do. It is more important than appearance, giftedness, or skill. It will make or break a company, a church, or a home. The remarkable thing is that we have a choice everyday regarding the attitude we will embrace for that day. We cannot change our past. Nor can we change the fact that people will act in a certain way. We also cannot change the inevitable. The only thing we can do is play on the one string we have, and that is our attitude. I am convinced that life is 10 percent what happens to me and 90 percent how I react to it. And so it is with you – we are in charge of our attitudes."*

At the age of 13, I lost my virginity and became a mother at the same time. I was an honor roll student but, when I was faced with a sex question, I gave the wrong answer. I said yes when I should have said no.

My school was in a state of shock. Their response was, *"What a shame. You are an honor roll student and now all you will be is just another negative welfare statistic."*

God was nowhere in my mind. However, He knew me and planted a positive attitude in my head that overshadowed the negative indictment against me. Although I didn't say it out loud. I said within myself, *"No. I'm better than that."*

To this end, I began to write the script for my life. Not the way it was, but the way I wanted it to be. There have been many twists and turns along the way, but I did graduate at the age of 16, on the honor roll, with a three-year-old son. And I've never been on welfare. In fact, I've started programs in my ministry to get young mothers off the welfare rolls. Importantly, God has blessed me to received recognition and honors from the city, county and state governments of Michigan, as well as from a former President of the United States for my community outreach work.

The point I'm trying to make here is what the Bible says, *"As a man thinketh in his heart, so is he"* (Proverbs 23:7a) At that time in my life, I didn't know that that was a Bible Scripture. So, if it worked for me, even more so, as Christians, we should expect it to work for us!

I am told that in golfer Arnold Palmer's office there is a plaque on his wall that reads as follows:

> **If you think you are beaten, you are**
> **If you think you dare not, you don't**
> **If you'd like to win but think you can't,**
> **It's almost certain you won't**
> **Life's battles don't always go**
> **To the stronger or faster man,**
> **But sooner or later, the man who wins**
> **Is the man who thinks he can.**

Stop the blame game. We are responsible for our attitudes.

The pessimist complains about the wind.

The optimist expects it to change.

The leader adjusts the sails.

How often have you heard people blaming others or circumstances for their behavior. It goes something like this:

If they are in a bad mood, they say, *"I got up on the wrong side of the bed this morning."*

If they experience failure, they say, *"I was born on the wrong side of the tracks."*

If they have successful family members, and they are not, they say, *"I was born in the wrong birth order."*

If their marriage fails, they say, *"I married the wrong person."*

If they miss a promotion, they say, *"I was in the wrong place at the wrong time."*

Friends, I encourage you to be brave enough to be willing to confront any necessary changes in your attitude. We must all be held accountable for our attitudes. There's something God wants us to get rid of. What is it you need to change? Don't ask yourself. Self probably won't tell you. Ask God. He will!

"Finally, brothers, whatsoever is true, whatsoever is right, whatsoever is noble, whatsoever is pure, whatsoever is lovely, whatsoever is admirable - if anything is excellent or praiseworthy - think about these things" **(Philipians 4:8).**

FEAR NOT

What is fear? To begin with, fear is a deadly emotion. The Bible says that in the last days man's hearts will fail them because of fear (Luke 21:26). Look around. There are plenty of reasons for one to fear were it not for our relationship with Jesus Christ and His promises, one of which is to keep us in perfect peace. (Isaiah 26:3)

Fear is having *"faith"* in the word that the enemy has spoken to us, individually, standing on it and waiting, knowing that it will come to pass. We do not do this knowingly; but that is what happens. When we believe the lies of the enemy, we find ourselves responding to people and to situations in such a way that our response actually brings about that thing which we fear. Job said, *"For what I fear comes upon me, and what I dread befalls me"* (Job 3:25).

Fear really is believing that the enemy is in control, and that he has as much, if not more power than God. Fear does not help us fight against the enemy. It agrees with him because he is the author of fear. It is not part of the armor of God described by Paul in Ephesians 6:11-17. Fear is the enemy's most deceptive weapon because we believe it is our human emotion.

Just this morning, prior to arising from a night's sleep, I was suddenly stirred awake by the loudest clap of thunder I've ever heard in my lifetime. Fear immediately gripped my heart. Truthfully speaking, my first thought was, *"God is mad and He is breaking through the sky and returning!"* My second thought was to hide. (I'm being very honest!) My third thought was, *"Why should I be afraid? Why should I hide? Surely, I want God to find me doing what I should be doing when He returns."*

I quickly recovered, and turned on the television to see what the newscasters had to say. Indeed, they gave a thunderstorm warning. I said my morning prayers and began my day with the peace of God that passes all understanding. (Philippians 4:7)

Fear is a universal emotion and has been around since the beginning of time. We first read about it in Genesis 3:10. It tells us that Adam was afraid when God spoke to him because he had sinned. Fear can be defined as the sensation that makes you believe that you are in danger and that something bad is about to happen.

There is an emotion of fear that is good. It is that which rises up within us when a rattlesnake slithers through the grass in front of our feet or when we hear an unfamiliar sound in the house in the middle of the night. It is what causes us to run from a burning building. This fear is self-preservation. Perhaps a respect for danger would best describe it. This could be called *"normal fear."* That is not what I am writing about here.

What are some of the symptoms of fear?

Of course, one of the first signs of fear is breathlessness.

However, there are many others:

- Heart fluttering (palpitations)
- Chest pain or pressure
- A sensation of suffocation or drowning
- Dizziness and vertigo
- A sensation of detachment from reality
- Tingling sensation in several parts of the body, heat or cold waves
- Sweating
- Dry mouth
- A sensation of fainting
- Trembling or shaking
- A fear of dying or becoming crazy, or losing control

There are many types of fear.

These are the top ten:

- Dying
- Lightening and thunder
- Cancer
- Heights

- Vomiting
- Closed places
- Open spaces
- Flying
- Social situations
- Spiders

FEAR, DREAD, AND WORRY ARE TRIPLETS

Another word for fear is dread. Dread steals joy. Dread comes for a two-fold purpose: to torment and to prevent. The devil uses dread to keep you from the blessings of God and to keep you out of His will.

Many times in the Bible when the Lord called people to do great things, He said, *"Fear not."* Fear is not from God.

> *"For God hath not given us the spirit of fear,*
> *but of power and of love and of a sound mind"*
> **(2 Timothy 1:7).**

Worry is fear. New things have a tendency to frighten us. We are afraid of the unknown. So we must pray about everything and fear nothing. The only thing we should fear is fear itself.

Faith is released through prayer. When fear comes knocking at the door, faith had better answer.

We need to watch for everything that steals our righteousness, our peace, and our joy. Talk back to the devil and experience more joy.

Fear is an aggressive enemy. It comes after us violently. We cannot be passive and defeat it. We are to be aggressive, if we are to fight an aggressive devil.

That's why it is urgently important to keep the Word of God in your mouth, in your ears and before your eyes.

When you use aggressive Christianity, you will experience victory. *"Ye are of God, little children, and have overcome them, because greater is He that is in you than he that is in the world"* (I John 4:4). But, if He that is in you is not exercised, then he that is in the world will overcome you. We need to be aggressive with the devil. Don't sit around and put up with his stuff!

When peace is leaving, you will feel worried or anxious, critical or judgmental. Pray. Pray right away. Come against that spirit. Say out loud, *"I will not be critical or judgmental. I will not judge anyone else. I have problems of my own. I do not have a wishbone. I have a backbone. I am not afraid of the devil. I resist him and he will flee from me. In all these things I am more than a conqueror."*

CAN WE LIVE WITHOUT FEAR?

Indeed, we can.

The Bible tells us, *"There is no fear in love; but perfect love casteth out fear, because fear hath torment. He that feareth is not made perfect in love"* (I John 4:18). I must admit that I'm still trying to get a better understanding of what *"perfect"* love really is. However, I do want to share some of the following insight with you. It is possible to live without fear. But, to do this, we must stand on the promises of God.

He has given us a holy covenant:

> *"The oath which he sware to our father Abraham, that he would grant unto us, that we being delivered out of the hand of our enemies might serve him without fear, in holiness and righteousness before him, all the days of our life"* **(Luke 1:68-75).**

Once we believe this promise, how do we obtain it? Simply put, we must not just love God, but we must love one another as Christ has loved us. How has He loved us? UNCONDITIONALLY! He loved us so much that He died for us. Are we willing to lay down our lives (flesh, own self-will) for our brothers and sisters in the Body of Christ, as well as sinners outside the Body of Christ? That includes those who have trespassed against us, abused, falsely accused, and betrayed us! That's not an easy thing to do. And, without the empowering help of the Holy Spirit, we can't do it alone. But, with God, all things are possible to those who believe (have faith).

We must also believe that God loves us:

> *"We have known and believed the love that God hath to us. God is love; and he that dwelleth in love dwelleth in God and God in him. Herein is our love made perfect, that we may have boldness in the day of*

*judgment; because as he is, so are we in this
world"* (I John 4:16-17).

If we doubt God's love for us, we live in torment.
"Fear has torment" (I John 4:18). Fear paralyses us and
keeps us from entering into the faith realm that God
desires us to live in.

Indeed, we're all under Satan's attack. But do not
fear. Be still. Do not push the panic button. Rest in the
knowledge that the Spirit of God is in you. He is the
Greater One. You will not go down. He has given His
angels charge over you.

His word says,

> *"Thou will keep him in perfect peace whose
> mind is stayed on thee, because he trusteth
> in thee. Trust ye in the Lord forever; for in
> the Lord Jehovah is everlasting strength"*
> **(Isaiah 26:3-4).**

Meditate on these Scriptures in both the Old and
New Testament regarding fear. There are many
others. These are just some of my favorite. Notice that
the Lord had to tell Joshua more than once not to be
afraid.

> *"And the LORD said unto Joshua, Fear not,
> neither be thou dismayed"* **(Joshua 8:1).**

> *"And the LORD said unto Joshua, Fear
> them not: for I have delivered them into
> thine hand; there shall not a man of them
> stand before thee"* **(Joshua 10:8).**

He also told women:

> *"And now, my daughter, fear not; I will do to thee all that thou requirest: for all the city of my people doth know that thou art a virtuous woman"* (Ruth 3:11).

> *"And the angel said unto her, Fear not, Mary: for thou hast found favour with God"* (Luke 1:30).

To others, He said:

> *"But Jesus heard it, he answered him, saying, Fear not: believe only, and she shall be made whole"* (Luke 8:50).

> *"Fear not, little flock; for it is your Father's good pleasure to give you the kingdom"* (Luke 12:32).

> *"But straightway Jesus spake unto them, saying, Be of good cheer; it is I; be not afraid"* (Matthew 14:27).

> *"These things I have spoken unto you, that in me ye might have peace. In the world ye shall have tribulation: but be of good cheer; I have overcome the world"* (John 16:33).

> *"For God hath not given us the spirit of fear; but of power, and of love, and of a sound mind"* (2 Timothy 1:7).

NOT ME!

By Casandria A. Sims

Twenty-five years ago I had been married for 15 years, with three children ages 13, 9, and 4. My husband was a hardworking, dedicated father with ambitions focusing on local politics. That was somewhat strange because, even though he was a great debater, he was not great at conversation and mingling. I never thought that today he would be a pastor and I would be a pastor's wife about to be ordained as a minister of the gospel of Jesus Christ.

Back then, we both were extremely shy and introverted, saddled with inferiority complexes, and found it hard to talk in front of a group of our peers. Yet, today when placed in our element speaking for Christ, we seem to transform into an alter-ego that finds little hardship in working with an audience to get the message across.

There was a time, during the first part of our 25 years in ministry, that I didn't know where I would have been had God, in His infinite wisdom, not shown me some things that built my faith for what was to come. There were many life experiences that lead to where I find myself today. Many of them interconnected but each developing a particular aspect of our lives and ministry.

To begin with, I did not come from a particularly religious background but my husband did. Both of his parents were strong Christians. His mother, Missionary Lillian G. Sims, was tenacious about the work of the Lord and made every effort to lead as many people as possible to Christ. I was no exception. But my attitude was, if he (my husband) wasn't getting saved, I wasn't either. However, after many years of following my mother-in-law around, listening to her teachings, watching her faith walk, and realizing the deep abiding sincerity and dedication she had, God was able to touch my heart and open my understanding. Praise the Lord. I got saved! That was the first milestone.

From that point on, I followed her with a different perspective of who I was and *"whose"* I am. Although I was a new person, I still felt uneasiness. I wanted so much for my husband to be saved also. Instead of being pushy, God gave me wisdom. I just put him on every prayer list I could. Within a year he was saved. That was the second milestone.

However, during the first few months of my husband's conversion, I began to question his sanity. He seemed to be having a nervous breakdown, becoming almost *"fanatical"* about his salvation. We had some very hard days, nights, weeks and months. My husband had such a quick and intense turn around that it was scary for me. At that time, I was ignorant of God's strategies. For months, all my husband could do was sleep (barely), eat (barely), go to work, pray (incessantly), cry (which was TOTALLY OUT OF CHARACTER), and go to church. I was on edge and at a loss for an explanation. I had prayed for his salvation and now that he was saved, I was questioning these strange behaviors. Was this the work of God or was this the effects of a nervous breakdown? I was afraid to speak to anyone in the church about what was going on and didn't know where to turn. So I had two personalities: The one I showed at work and church and the fearful one that dominated my home life.

Then, just as quickly as it came, the effects of his change began to subside. We were finally settling into a calmer, more relaxed atmosphere. During these months, my husband became very active in the church and poured himself into the work of the Lord. Just as I thought we were finally where God wanted us to be (I was happy), my husband dropped a bombshell on me. He came to me and said he thought God wanted him to be a minister. My mouth opened slightly and my eyes showed compassion. I reacted to him as a supportive wife, but on the inside I was hysterical. *"NO, NO, NO! You don't want to be a minister. You can hardly talk to me; you can't talk and mingle well with the people on your job. (We'd been to some social events sponsored by his job and he demonstrated the epitome of a social cripple.) How is God calling YOU to be a minister?"* In my prayer one night, and many more to come, I said to God, *"God, all I asked you to do was to save him! What's all this minister stuff?"*

Now that we were both saved, God's call to my husband to become a minister was the next life changing experience. It began another few months of turmoil in my life. I had questioned his ability to be a minister, though I never said it to his face. However, the major problem I had was what would be expected of *"me"* as a minister's wife? I was comfortable working in the church office and serving on the usher board. You didn't have to talk or present in front of anybody to do those jobs. No one would ask me to step out and do anything out of my realm of comfort. I saw what minister's wives had to do and what was expected of them. That disturbed me. Additionally, I could almost stay where I was (as far as my growth was concerned), and still be a *"good Christian."*

My husband says it was hard for him to acknowledge this ministerial calling upon his life to me but it was even harder to confess it to our pastor, especially since he'd only been saved less than a full year. I could hear him in the basement preaching to the walls. His prayers were so loud and so fervent until one neighbor in particular would call me over, make comments, and ask questions about what was going on with him. Now I know that all of this was the conviction God had on my husband to acknowledge his calling to the ministry, because as soon as he did, our lives became normal again. That is to say that the obsessive preaching and praying was no longer consuming him.

After getting over the initial shock, I said to God, *"Okay, whatever you want me to do, I'll do it."* Then God began to quell some of my fears and I slowly began to take on my *"role"* as a minister's wife.

Yet again, I began to notice something different in my husband. There was a sense of *"unsettlement"* about him. He seemed to be uncomfortable and unfocused. I didn't have to wait long before he began to share with me some of the things God was telling him. An alarm went off on my insides! All of his talk seemed to point to moving out and starting a church. Our children loved going to the church we were presently attending. They were in the Youth Choir and active in the Youth Department. We were comfortable at Calvary Church of God in Christ. My spirit, or should I say my natural self, kept praying *"No, No, No!"*

Once again, we had a traumatic experience to deal with. How strange is it now to say that an assignment given by God can be classified as a traumatic experience? However, at that time that was my feeling, even though I thought I now had a close walk with God. I thought how you (Henry) dare disturb this picture perfect family worship experience. I had seen the struggles of my pastor (and he had an established church) and those in our jurisdiction who had begun a work for God. (Oh No! Not Me! Notice how that *"me"* keeps coming up). My heart dropped as he finally voiced those words to me. He had now gained enough confidence, once again, to tell our pastor. Here we go into the wilderness again!

Let me fast forward here, our pastor, Elder James E. Slappy, Jr., was very supportive. We didn't leave overnight. We set a one-year period before we left. During that time, replacements were found for my husband's position as Youth Minister, his place on the Youth Advisory Board, and his Sunday School Class. We became just regular members. We did not stop our financial support, yet we were able to save for our own church. This savings plan was another one laid out by God.

Even though everyone now knew we were going to be leaving, and we ourselves accepted the fact that we would be separating from our church home, the transition did not come easy. When the time came, there were lots of tears and fears from both my children and myself. However, I had learned by then how to say, *"Ok God, whatever it is you want me to do, I'll do,"* and I believe my mourning time was cut shorter.

And so here we are! I believe that had it not been for faith; first the faith God had in us, and secondly the faith we developed during those hard times, neither of us would be who we are today. Shortly, I will become a licensed minister. Me, the skinny girl called *"Olive Oil,"* with Bugs Bunny teeth; the girl that shied away from crowds; the one who could not look into the face of others, and who became physically ill when placed in front of a group of my peers to speak. Me! Proclaiming the gospel of Christ. Me, who enjoyed and still enjoys working behind the scene, becoming a minister. Well, I guess if God

can use a donkey to speak (Numbers 22), He can
certainly use me. But who would ever think it?

*Casandria Sims was born in Tennessee but has lived
in Detroit, Michigan for nearly 37 years. She earned
a Bachelors Degree from Middle Tennessee State
University and a Masters Degree from Wayne State
University. She and husband Henry have been
married for almost 41 years. They have four adult
children. Casandria was employed by the Detroit
Board of Education as a teacher until retiring in
2004. She is now employed by the Lord.*

TRUST THE LORD

*"Trust the Lord with all of your heart and
lean not unto your own understanding. In
all thy ways acknowledge Him and He will
direct your path"* **(Proverbs 3:5-6).**

We get in trouble when we put more trust in
ourselves than we do in God. God is omnipotent (all
mighty); omnipresent (everywhere); omniscient (all
knowing). We are none of these.

Some folks put more faith in objects and people
they don't know than they do in God. For example,
when you are about to sit in a chair you don't shake
the chair or check out its legs to be sure it is strong
enough to hold you up! No. You sit right down in it
without a second thought.

Another example is when you drive your car down the street. You trust that when the light is green the other cars that are stopped at the red light will let you safely proceed. You don't stop the car, get out in the middle of the street, wave your arms and ask the other drivers, *"Are you going to stop and let me go?"* Isn't that thought absurd? Why can't we trust God at least as much as someone we don't know or a chair!

"It is better to trust in the LORD than to put confidence in man" (Psalm 118:8).

Let me give you an example of this. I know a lady who had prayed and prayed that God would give her a boy when she was pregnant. In fact, she got into the realm of begging. Her husband wanted a boy. Her other children wanted a little brother. She was sure that God wouldn't disappoint all of the family.

To this woman's utter amazement, when she delivered a healthy baby girl, she was sorely disappointed. *"God, how could you do this?"* She asked. *"You said if we just believe, we shall receive. Well, I believed you for a little boy. What happened?"* What happened, is this:

This lady had more *confidence in her own prayers* than she had *faith* in God. She was seeing through a glass darkly (I Corinthians 13:12). But God knows best and surely had His reasons for sending a little girl rather than the little boy that was prayed for. Perhaps one day this mother will understand that God is sovereign. It's best when we pray, and make our request known unto God, that we conclude our prayers with, *"Lord, let thy will be done."*

This reminds me of the scenario of Jesus being in the Garden of Gethsame. He didn't want to be crucified, but this is what He said,

> *"And he went a little farther, and fell on his face, and prayed, saying, O my Father, if it be possible, let this cup pass from me: nevertheless not as I will, but as thou wilt"* (Matthew 26:39).

In his book, *Let Us Pray*, Watchman Nee says, *"A spirit of trust is most essential to prayer and to the total Christian life. If our relationship with the Lord continually fluctuates with our having neither assurance nor confidence, our entire life will be fatally wounded."*

True trust is based on one factor, which is Christ Himself. In Jesus Name, we may come boldly to the Father at anytime and anywhere.

> *"Having therefore, brethren, boldness to enter into the Holy place by the blood of Jesus, by the way which he dedicated for us, a new and living way...and having a great priest...let us draw near with a true heart in fullness of faith"* (Hebrews 10:19-22).

Man's wisdom is foolishness to God. (1 Corinthians 3:19). When our faith is put in the wrong person and things don't go our way, we blame God. What we need to do is obey God and leave the consequences to Him. Even Confucius says, *"Real knowledge is to know the extent of one's ignorance."*

Finally, I like what Job said, *"Though He slay me, yet will I trust Him"* (Job 13:15). Friends, we are talking about trusting God enough to totally surrender!

REHEARSE YOUR VICTORIES

Some of us are absent-minded professors. We confess that we are believers, that we trust God, but we are forgetful! If you feel yourself losing faith, it's time for a trip down memory lane. Think back about times in the past when God brought you through a major challenge. He did it before. He will do it again. He promised!

One of the biggest faith killers is television. Cut it off! Who needs to be constantly reminded that millions have lost their jobs, billions of dollars have been lost in the stock market, hundreds of thousands of homes have been foreclosed, countries are warring against each other, homicides are occurring every minute, and trillions of dollars for our future have been spent.

Up until last year, when I was a news junkie, I had cable television on in two rooms. All day long too much negative information was getting into my mind. One day I decided to discontinue my cable service. However, before I did, they discontinued it for me for lack of payment, They did me a favor. I found out that I CAN live without it. In fact, I can live BETTER without it! The money saved can now be used for something much more edifying. (Like a good book!)

FIRE-PROOF FAITH

God wants us to have *"fire-proof faith."* Indeed, we are in the fiery furnace, and our adversary has turned up the heat. Therefore, we must likewise fight the good fight of faith. (I Timothy 6:12). Thanks go to Mrs. Wanda Burnside, president of The Called and Ready Writers for this poignant poem. Let it bless you.

BY FIRE

By Wanda J. Burnside

Are you at a point in your life where all you seem to have are disappointments, frustrations and suffering? Does it seem like no matter how hard you try, things just don't turn out the way you feel they should? You prayed and prayed, but it seems like one thing after another just keeps happening to you.

You cried out to the Lord, *"Why is this and that happening to me? I am seeking Your face, Father! What am I to do? Things are so painful in my life. Lord, do you hear my cry? Do You care that I am going through one thing then another?"*

GOD IS THERE! He hears your cry. Listen, listen to what He has to say. Open your heart.

Wait on Him.

Yes, you are in the fire, saith the Lord:

I am perfecting you. I am making you into what you must be to succeed and survive in this life.

I am changing you. I am taking out all that is not pure and right. I want you to be holy.

I want you to be "wholly" and completely mine. I want you to function and operate as I have made you to be.

You feel the heat of the fire. You are in the process of being changed. I have chosen you. I have picked you up and brought you near the fire to be changed and purified of this world. I don't want worldly ways in your life. I don't want the world to come into your life and contaminate you. There must not be pollution in your spirit.

You hear the crackling of the fire. This is the trouble and the problems that seemed to just pop up in your life. They are now being dealt with by the flames of My holy fire. They are like wood. I will handle them.

It is now time to come closer to the fire. I have selected you. I picked you. I have carried you to this place. I have brought you closer. You are getting closer to Me.

I need you! I want to use you. I have set you aside for My use and service. I have called you. Just like My children, the Israelites, who traveled by fire, you will too. It will be light to your path and warmth to your heart.

I send the fire! I am the Master of the fire! I

control its temperature. I set the gauge. I control it all. You will not burn or be consumed. I love you. I need you to be perfected for My service.

I need a pure heart.

I want a humble spirit.

I must dwell in a clean temple.

You are a holy temple.

My Spirit will clean this temple!

I want your life in order.

I dwell in order!

I deserve praise for I will make your life free from bondage. The ropes of bondage will burn off by My fire.

Worship Me!

Worship Me!

Worship Me!

Copyright 2008

For other gospel tracts, poetry, books and products you can contact:

Wanda J. Burnside, Founder and President
Write the Vision Ministries and Productions, International
P. O. Box 125, Dearborn, MI 48121-0125
Email: wtvision@hotmail.com
Website: www.thecalledandreadywriters.org

TIMING

Often times, one loses faith because they have implemented poor timing. God has a time and a season for all things. We must understand that when to make a move is as important as what to do and how to do it. We must avoid taking the wrong action at the wrong time and taking the right action at the wrong time. God will show us the right action at the right time leading to success.

Ecclesiastes 3:1-8

For everything there is a season,
And a time for every matter under heaven:
A time to be born, and a time to die;
A time to plant, and a time to pluck up what is planted;
A time to kill, and a time to heal;
A time to break down, and a time to build up;
A time to weep, and a time to laugh;
A time to mourn, and a time to dance;
A time to throw away stones, and a time to gather stones together;
A time to embrace, And a time to refrain from embracing;
A time to seek, and a time to lose;
A time to keep, and a time to throw away;
A time to tear, and a time to sew;
A time to keep silence, and a time to speak;
A time to love, and a time to hate,
A time for war, and a time for peace.

You have heard it said that God is never late. I agree. But sometimes it sure seems like He is last minute! Nevertheless, I've learned over the years that God's time is always the right time. Lord, teach us to wait.

PATIENCE

Timing requires patience. Indeed, patience is a virtue. This speaks of the importance of a particular personal attribute. The word *"virtue"* means the quality of doing what is right and avoiding what is wrong.

We are living in an Instant Age and many are falling into a deep pit. This happens when we refuse to wait on God and instead become self-reliant, and seek instant results with our own actions. Although we may not voice it, our actions indicate, *"I want my way and I want it now! I will determine my future course and make it happen."* Friends, we are not the masters of our own future. We can see down the street, but God can see around the corner.

Our sighs and groans signal impatience and discontent. Grumbling about people is a thinly veiled way of complaining about God.

The Israelites had been enslaved in Egypt for hundreds of years. Then God sent a deliverer, Moses, who wasn't any too happy himself to be in that role. But he went. No sooner then he began to obey God, however, people began to complain. He went to

Pharaoh with God's message and came away with no more than the command that the Hebrews had to find their own straw to make bricks (Exodus 5). The people blamed him. Once the people were free – and hemmed in by the Red Sea – they complained again (Exodus 14). Each time the Lord brought them through one victory they rejoiced. But, as soon as another problem came, they grumbled again. They complained about lack of meat; God sent quail (Exodus 16). They complained about thirst; God brought water out of the rock (Exodus 17). It went on that way for 40 years. Problem, grumble. Problem, complain. Paul wrote about this generation of Israelites

> *"Now these things occurred as examples to keep us from setting our hearts on evil things as they did.... And do not grumble, as some of them did -- and were killed by the destroying angel"* (1 Corinthians 10:6, 10).

> *"Do everything without complaining or arguing, so that you may become blameless and pure, children of God without fault in a crooked and depraved generation, in which you shine like stars in the universe"* (Philippians 2:14-16).

Moses said with great insight,

> *"You are not grumbling against us, but against the Lord"* (Exodus 16:8).

I like this quote by our esteemed President, Barack Obama, which speaks about patience.

"Making your mark on the world is hard. If it were easy, everybody would do it. But it's not. It takes patience, it takes commitment, and it comes with plenty of failure along the way. The real test is not whether you avoid this failure, because you won't. It's whether you let it harden or shame you into inaction, or whether you learn from it; whether you choose to persevere."

June 16, 2006 - Evanston, IL
Northwestern University Commencement Address

"As you know, we consider blessed those who have persevered. You have heard of Job's perseverance and have seen what the Lord finally brought about. The Lord is full of compassion and mercy" **(James 5:12).**

The following is an excerpt from one of my books, *At His Feet:*

STAY IN LINE

If you have been waiting for what seems like an eternity for God to answer a particular prayer request, your faith is evaporating, and you are starting to become weary from waiting, this visual aid is especially for you.

I want you to see a long line similar to what we wait in at the supermarket or bank. See yourself somewhere in the middle. At the front of that line is God's storehouse of blessings with your name on many of them. The Precious Savior Himself is there overseeing the storehouse. Hear Him saying:

"Don't be weary. Stay in line. As each person in front of you moves up to claim his or her blessings, rejoice for them. Rejoice also because you get to move up a step or two. Don't murmur or complain and say, "'What about me, Lord? I'm your faithful servant too. I've even been serving you longer than she has."

Hear the Lord saying, *"Stop comparing yourself with the faithfulness of others. Serve Me with a pure heart. No good thing will I withhold from them who walk upright before me."*

He continues, *"Furthermore, don't be distracted by what's going on along the sidelines. Those are Satan's devices to snare you and to get your eyes off the mark. Look straight ahead and stay in line. Remember what happens when you get out of the grocery store line. You lose your place and have to go to the end and start over again. This happens to many of My people, and that's why it seems as though I am not responding to their prayers. Also, there are times when My people become distracted by what's happening on the sidelines and they don't realize that the person in front of them has moved up. So the person behind them goes around the distracted one. This also can delay your blessings.*

"Remember also that there are no shortcuts in this line, but you can make the time seem shorter

by waiting patiently for your turn. Most of all, remember that My Son, Jesus Christ, is the author and finisher of your faith. He also is waiting. He's waiting for you to get to the front of the line."

I truly appreciate the Lord's speaking to my heart. Let Him likewise speak to yours. Persevere, my friends. Stay in line. Rejoice with them who rejoice. Your blessing could be just a step away.

I CAN WAIT

I've heard it, and you have too
"Patience is a virtue"
No one likes to wait
No one likes to hesitate
The world says,
"He who hesitates is lost"
But I decided to count the cost
If I want to be a part of God's flock
I must stay on His time clock
For when I get ahead of the Good Shepherd
I miss my instructions and can't hear a word
I begin to stumble and fall
Because I miss His love call
So, ask me again, Can I wait?
You bet I can. He's never late!

Minister Mary Edwards

HOW TO GET A PRAYER BREAKTHROUGH

Next to writing, my favorite thing to do is to listen to music. In fact, the two just go together for me.

As I sit here writing, the lyrics to the song, *"I Almost Gave Up,"* are bouncing through the air and have landed on my eardrums. I can relate to these words. Perhaps you can too.

Sometimes life gets so tough that even the most faith-filled Christian has difficulty stirring up enough faith to pray for a breakthrough. More than once I've cried out to the Lord, *"Father, give me a breakthrough before I have a breakdown!"*

Over the years, however, I have found these to be times when God wants to take my faith to a whole new level. During these stressful times, there are lessons to be learned before we throw in the towel.

Lesson number one, we must believe that there is no problem too hard, too big, or too difficult for our God. Instead of coming boldly to the throne of grace as we have been instructed by God to do, we worry, complain, live in fear, doubt, depression, and ask our friends for advice. We pray what I call "worry prayers." I heard someone say, *"If you are going to pray, don't worry. And if you are going to worry, don't pray."*

The second lesson we need to learn is to patiently wait for our answer. We want God to hurry up. *"What's taking Him so long? If He can do anything, why doesn't He just go ahead and do it? Does He really hear me when I cry? Does He care about my problems?"*

Why do we pray? Is it just to get answers from God? If we pray only because we want answers from God, we will get irritated and angry with God, especially when the answer doesn't come the way we want it to come. God wants us to come to Him in prayer because He desires intimacy (in to me see) with us. Too many of our prayers are *"Give me, give me, give me."*

I'm going to stop right now and ask God to magnify your sanctified imagination and see how big He is. Do you realize that heaven is His throne and earth is His footstool? (Isaiah 66:1). Think about this:

The next time you are faced with an insurmountable problem, I want you to look into the heavens on a clear night. The evidence of God's greatness is right above your head. Scientists say that there are 7,000 stars visible to the naked eye, though only about 2,000 of these can be seen at any one time and place. So even on the clearest night you can only see a third of all the stars visible to people all over the world. But that's not the end of it. Recent studies indicate that there are far more stars than the eye can see, perhaps 200 billion – that's 200,000,000,000 – in our own galaxy, and the Milky Way is just one of millions of galaxies! Though no one knows exactly how many stars there are, one estimate puts the number at three thousand million billion stars – a three with sixteen zeros behind it. That's a lot of stars to say the least!

God wants us to know that His answers are always worth waiting for.

> *"Something should remind us once more that the great things in this universe are things we never see. You walk out at night and look up at the beautiful stars as they bedeck the heavens like swinging lanterns of eternity, and you think you can see all. Oh, no. You can never see the law of gravitation that holds them there"*
> **(Dr. Martin Luther King, Jr.)**

King David was so sure of God's faithfulness that he wrote, *"My soul, wait patiently for God alone, for my expectation is from Him"* (Psalm 62:5 NKJV).

God wants us to know that His answers are always worth waiting for. Friend, divine delay brings greater glory.

We must spend time on our knees getting direction from God. I call this *"Knee"*ology, not *"Me"*ology. At the end of our prayers, we say, *"Thy will be done."* We must surrender to His will and trust that He knows what's best for us. Remember, when we put the decision in His hands, if we don't take the credit when things turn out the way we prayed that they would, we don't have to take the blame if things *"appear"* to go wrong.

CLOSE THE DOOR

By Rev. Marva Stafford

*"But thou, when thou prayest enter into thy
closet, and when thou hast shut thy door,
pray to thy Father which is in secret; and
thy Father which seeth in secret shall
reward thee openly"* (Matthew 6:6).

While praying to my Father, I realized that I
was thinking about my school homework
assignment. My mind was wandering. My focus
was off God. It occurred to me that this
happened often when I entered my prayer
closet.

After this last episode, I tried to concentrate
more on my communications with God. How
can I keep my communications with God from
being broken? These distractions were as
though I was walking out the door when God
wanted to speak to me.

I realized that the adversary was trying to
keep me away from my help, my strength, and
my guidance. This situation was causing me
great distress. My faith and my closeness with
the Lord were being attacked.

Then one day I was looking through a book
of prayers that was given to me by a co-worker.

In hopes of finding inspiration to help someone else who was depressed about her trials and pain, I found my help in Matthew 6:6. The Scripture was so clear; I understood exactly what was happening to me. So simple, I forgot to close the door as I prayed. I left the door wide open and the enemy filled my mind with my worries, my issues, my doubts, my fears, my illness, how do I look, lack of confidence, my worthlessness, and lack of trust.

Soon after this revelation, I preached Matthew 6:6. I know the sermon helped many people who heard with a spiritual ear from the Lord that Sunday morning. It still helps me this very day. I know that I must always focus on the Lord when I am in a conversation with Him. I must use my measure of faith by believing that He hears me and I hear Him. And, when I go into my prayer closet, I must CLOSE THE DOOR.

Marva Stafford lives in Oak Park, Michigan, daughter of Essie Stafford. She is a servant of God, preacher, teacher, poet and author. Rev. Marva writes to express the love of Christ to everyone. She serves in many capacities and is a board member of The Called and Ready Writers in Detroit.

Email: MBless211@aol.com

There is also a time to open the door. In his book, *My Utmost For His Highest*, Oswald Chambers says, *"Unless you learn how to open the door of your life completely and let God in from your first waking moment of each new day, you will be working on the wrong level throughout the day. But if you will swing the door fully open and pray to your Father who is in secret, every public thing in your life will be marked with the lasting imprint of the presence of God."*

Finally, and perhaps this should be first, we should ask Jesus to teach us how to pray (Matthew 5). Too often we go into the prayer closet and want to do all of the talking. Be still and listen to the voice of the Lord. Meditate on what you want to say to Him so that what you say makes some sense. Life and death are in the power of the tongue – and prayer! (Proverbs 18:21).

DISCIPLINE

I love me some nice, cold, sweet watermelon in the hot days of summer. *"Okay. Minister Mary, what does that have to do with discipline?"* I'm so glad you asked.

The problem is salt. Eating watermelon without salt just isn't the same as eating it with salt. Salt seems to give it just the right touch and is palatable to my taste buds. However, there's iodine in salt and I'm allergic to iodine. Salt isn't good for my blood pressure and it causes my feet to swell. This reminds me of the Scripture that says, *"It is like leaven, which a woman took and hid in three measures of meal until the whole was leavened"* (Luke 13:21). Even though I know this, I have a serious challenge when it comes to leaving the salt alone. I need more discipline in this area.

Since I'm in a confession mode, let me tell you this. My discipline isn't nearly as good as it was when I was married. Then I was accountable to someone that I had to live in peace with. I made necessary adjustments. I went to bed early and rose up early in the morning. Ben Franklin said, *"Early to bed, early to rise, makes one healthy, wealthy and wise."* Guess that's why my ship hasn't come in yet. I'm staying up too late!

Exercise. This is not one of my favorite things to do. In fact, the only real exercise I get is in physical therapy for my leg. I'm suppose to go three times a week. But, I do good when I get there twice. I always have a good excuse for not going. At least I think it's a good one. In reality, it's lack of discipline. Usually my excuse is sitting in front of the computer writing. That's what I really enjoy doing.

Rest. Let me give you a definition of rest, since most of us have no idea of what rest is. (I had to look it up myself.) Rest is defined as a lack of motion. Another understanding of rest is the state of peace. A consequence of the meaning normally associated with rest is a ceasing from work, activity or from sleep. For some, rest is equated to halting all motions and thus becoming free from anxiety and distress. Many liken rest to death, when all activity has ceased forever on this side of life. Sure, when we go to heaven our souls will rest in peace. But God wants us to learn how to rest while we are here on earth. However, most of us don't know how to rest. Even when we attempt to be still our minds are busy. We are either thinking about what we just did or what we are going to do next. In fact, some of us feel guilty if we are not busy!

In her book, *Rest is a Spiritual Thing*, Pastor P.K. Roberts says, *"Rest and derivatives of rest are mentioned 307 times in the Bible. For God to mention it that many times, it must be important."* She goes on to say, *"If we are to truly rest, we must cultivate a soft heart toward God. To do this, we must give attention daily to allowing our Father to turn the soil of our hearts in whatever way He sees fit."*

Anyway, the point that I'm trying to make is this: God wants us to be balanced people. He desires discipline. He wants us to eat right, sleep sweet, exercise these bodies, and rest in Him.

> *"And he said unto them, Come ye yourselves apart into a desert place, and rest a while; for there were many coming and going, and they had no leisure so much as to eat"* **(Mark 6:31).**

Sometimes we are so tired that our bodies, minds, and eventually our faith all weaken. God don't get no glory out of tired saints who can't think straight and don't do right.

Let me close with a definition of spiritual discipline. It can be described as a habit or regular pattern in your life that repeatedly brings you back to God and opens you up to what God is saying to you. It keeps our relationship with God in good working order and even helps develop intimacy. There is a time for work and a time for rest. A time to lead and take action; a time to let the Spirit lead, and a time to sit still and listen to the Voice of God. Practice makes perfect. We must also be open to rebuke from the Lord when we stray from His ways. *"My son, do not despise the chastenings of the Lord, nor be discouraged when you are rebuked by Him"* (Hebrews 12:5). Simply put, NO POUTING.

JOY

"Then he (Nehemiah) said unto them, Go your way, eat the fat, and drink the sweet, and send portions unto them for whom nothing is prepared. For this day is holy unto the Lord: neither be ye sorry; for the joy of the Lord is your strength"
(Nehemiah 8:10).

"Whatever happened to that joyful woman I married?"

This penetrating question was asked to me by my late husband, Rev. Eddie K. Edwards. I didn't have an answer.

For 10 years, I had served as the ministry's Development Director, a/k/a fundraiser. A major part of my responsibility was to help raise at least $1,000,000 dollars a year for Joy of Jesus Ministries. Because of the stress associated with trying to raise this much money, I had lost my joy. Most development directors only hold this position for seven years. I had clearly overstayed my time. Could that be the reason my joy had evaporated? I was soon to find out when I went into my secret closet to pray.

"Lord, what has happened to my joy?" I asked. His brief response was, *"You let the work smother your joy."* Indeed, I had.

What happened to me so often happens to those who work in ministry – especially when you are the *"first lady."* You live in a glass house with no fire escape anywhere in sight. The ministry is your day job, your afternoon job, and your night job. You feel like everyone wants your blood and no one is checking the gauge. There are days when you feel like a juggler in a circus. The adversary had plucked the fruit of joy right out of my life.

One day I looked up and made a horrible and frightening discovery. The fruit of joy wasn't the only fruit of the spirit, (Galatians 5:22), that was missing. Along with it went my peace and my patience. My love for my ministry also was slowly slipping away.

Take heed my friends. God loves a cheerful giver. (2 Corinthians 9:7). When you find that you can no longer be a cheerful giver, it's definitely time to stop and evaluate. Ask yourself, *"Where has my joy gone? How did I let that happen? And, what can I do to regain it?"*

While this book doesn't allow me the room to expound to the degree I desire on why we lose our joy, suffice it to say that we have been commanded to rejoice in the Lord always. (Philippians 4:4). Be of good cheer. (Matthews 9:2). And to not let our hearts be troubled. (St. John 14:1).

I fell under heavy conviction when the Lord told me that I *"allowed"* the enemy to steal my joy. It could have and should have been prevented before I was asked that soul-searching question. So, make monitoring your joy a part of your life style.

We so often hear the closing words of the above cited passage, *"...for the joy of the Lord is your strength."* But, in reality, it takes on an even deeper, richer meaning. Joy comes from knowing how to serve God better and without becoming bitter.

Approaching this subject from another perspective: *"Without a vision, the people perish"* (Proverbs 29:18). When a person has no vision, he has no reason to get out of bed in the morning. Why take the next step when you don't have a destination? All you have waiting for you are the same trivial tasks that you did yesterday. If this is you, you need to ask God, *"Why was I born?"* He will show you your intended purpose. I can say with certainty that once you know that, you can approach each new day with joy. When you know your purpose in life, you will be able to say as Paul said, *"I am exceedingly joyful in all of our tribulation"* (2 Corinthians 7:4). Let me add that once we know our mission and how it fits into God's *"heavenly vision"* (spoken of in Acts 26:19), we must be obedient to it – no matter what comes up or what goes down.

When I meditate on the joy of the Lord, often the smiling face that comes before me is my neighbor, Dr. Wilma Robena Johnson, pastor of New Prospect Baptist Church.

Before I met Pastor Johnson (Pastor J) in person, I met her in the spirit 11 years ago. When Pastor J was being considered to become the first female pastor of New Prospect, I joined a team of prayer warriors led by the late Brenda Johnson (not related to Pastor J) to soak this decision in prayer. Although this wasn't my church home, I felt compelled to be a part of this prayer group.

I'm happy to report that the church made a very wise decision and selected Pastor J. I'm even happier to report that they have had absolutely no regrets. Pastor J has taken her congregation and this community to a whole new level.

Finally I met Pastor J at her installation in 1999, and I'm blessed to report that I was honored to be New Prospect's first prayer breakfast speaker the next year when the prayer group invited me to come.

Pastor J leads her congregation with spiritual joy. She describes what this is in her book, *Giving Away My Joy*. It's a commentary on pastoral leadership. I highly recommend it as an excellent example for leaders to follow.

Recently, Pastor J celebrated her 10th anniversary as pastor of the church. It was a great celebration. However, immediately afterwards, she fell and broke her foot. Satan tried to trip her up. Instead, she tripped him up. Satan didn't get the victory. She continued her joy journey. In fact, she allowed Widows With Wisdom, my support group for women who must learn how to live without their spouses, to use the church's community center during our meeting. Lo and behold, in hobbles Pastor J to greet us with a big smile and a hearty hug! As the saying goes, *"You can't keep a good woman down."*

I've shared this story with you to show how we can let the work of the Lord smother us to death and steal our joy. Or, we can allow it to inspire, invigorate, and bring life to those around us. Pastor J, I salute you!

Part Three

89

Part Three

Part Three

A GREAT CLOUD OF WITNESSES

"Therefore, seeing we also are compassed about by so great a cloud of witnesses, let us lay aside every weight, and the sin which doth so easily beset us, and let us run with patience the race that is set before us"
(Hebrews 12:1).

"And they overcame him by the blood of the Lamb and by the word of their testimony, and they loved not their lives unto the death" **(Revelation 12:11).**

There are no adjectives to adequately describe the great joy I have had in writing this book. Quite frankly, I never would have chosen *"faith"* as my topic. It was assigned to me by the Holy Spirit. Let me share with you how it came about.

In May of this year, I was asked by a publishing company to write a book on faith. It would be released in time for the Thanksgiving and Christmas holidays when so many people slip into depression for various reasons.

Realizing how helpful this topic could be, I got very excited. This book was written under a heavy anointing. It was done in four days! (*"Something"* got a hold of me!) I couldn't stop writing. Day and night. Night and day. Without knowing it, I was on a fast. I didn't even want food. When I went to bed at night, I couldn't sleep. Words to write crowded my head. I would get up in the middle of the night and turn on my computer. There was a great sense of urgency in my spirit to get the book done.

After completing three-quarters of the book, and sharing it with the project managers for the publishing company, they informed me that the book was too *"one-sided"* (Jesus). And they wanted me to give the readers who were not Christians other *"Higher Power Options."* I think these people have lost their mind. Perhaps that's the problem. They are operating with their own mind! Someone needed to tell them that there IS no higher power than Jesus Christ. I was the one to let them know. God's word will not return to Him void.

I emphasized my beliefs to the publishers and asked to be out of the contract. Compromising wasn't even an option for me. They agreed. Strangely enough, I wasn't the least bit disappointed. In fact, I'm excited. Jesus let me know that I wrote the manuscript especially for the project managers who need to be saved. They told me that they read every word of it. PTL! I'm claiming these souls for Jesus.

Immediately after this incident, the Lord informed me that He wanted me to self-publish the book, as I have all my others.

He even gave me a new name for it:

FAITH: USE IT OR LOSE IT!

Many people, saved and unsaved, are hurting. They are walking around in a fog, overwhelmed with the problems and trials thrust upon them. Some have stopped praying and can't even concentrate on reading the Bible. I believe this easy-to-read book will strengthen the readers' faith and they will be able to fight the good fight of faith, which we are commanded to do in I Timothy 6:12, *"Fight the good fight of faith. Lay hold on eternal life, whereunto thou art also called and hast professed a good profession before many witnesses."*

It is my prayer that what you have already read will edify and encourage you. The following stories are written by overcomers. They are standing on God's promises and keeping the faith by the words of their testimonies. (Revelations 12:11).

Let me begin with another one of my personal stories of faith.

The Buck Stops Here
By Minister Mary Edwards

CANCER: First my mother. Then my brother. Followed by my sister. All in 18 months. Whew! Finally, a breather. But only for two years before my beloved husband was stricken.

Prior to my late husband's departure, we had been community activist in Detroit for over 30 years. He loved Detroit and everyone knew it. So often we heard him say, "*I was born here. Raised here, and I will die here.*"

Strangely enough, following his retirement in 2002, he said, "*I believe I can leave Detroit now.*" We were all amazed. Rev. Eddie K. Edwards had been a Michiganian of the Year, received a Presidential Award for his community service and was highly regarded by the city, state, and county governments for his commitment to Michigan. More importantly, most of our family live here. This sudden change of heart was hard for us to understand. Nevertheless, in December 2003, we began to make plans to relocate to Texas.

During the Christmas season, we looked for a home in Texas. It didn't take long for us to find a lovely one. Negotiations began on the purchase, pending the sale of our Detroit home. We rushed back and put our home on the market. The real estate agent we worked with felt sure our home would sell quickly. We were all surprised when 30 people looked at the home and, even though many expressed their love for it, not one put a bid on it. Thank God they didn't.

In March 2004, Eddie began to complain about having a pain in his side. At first, the doctor diagnosed it as an infection and gave him a prescription for antibiotics, which he took for about a month. When his condition didn't improve, he had a biopsy. That's when we discovered that he was in stage four of cancer and only had four to six months of life left! He was a health-conscious person and it was difficult for us to understand how his condition could develop to stage four without us knowing something was so terribly wrong. He left this life in July 2004, just five months after his diagnosis.

My husband's passing left me in a state of utter shock about the need to make important decisions alone. But the transition from wife to widow wasn't the only major crisis I had to deal with. Before I could catch my breath, I WAS DIAGNOSED WITH CANCER MYSELF. I've always been faithful to have my mammograms on a consistent basis. Upon having my annual mammogram, the test showed something *"abnormal"* was on the film. I needed to have a biopsy, which I did. The biopsy came back stage one of breast cancer. Naturally, I was panic-stricken. Images of death began to dance in my head. I thought about my mother, my brother, my sister, and my husband – all dying from this awful disease.

Once I got over my initial fears, I rose up and prepared myself for battle. I have always been a fighter and it's a good thing. Now I was fighting for my OWN life and the life of my grandchildren and great grandchildren. ENOUGH IS ENOUGH! I refused to sit idly by and watch this deadly disease take the lives of my offspring.

Being a writer, I have a very creative imagination. Immediately, I began to see myself healed – instead of dead. Instead of writing out my obituary, I wrote out my goals for the next five years. And I wrote my autobiography. I also designed and posted signs all over my home for my eyes to see. One of the signs said: *"THE BUCK STOPS HERE!"* Below is another sign. I've also shared this image with others going through cancer challenges. I hope it will help someone else. *(The sign depicts CANCER with the 'R' crossed out and replaced with an 'L')*

When it came time for my scheduled surgery, I can truthfully say that all fear was gone. Although I had to go back twice for the disease to be removed, (it was so small that it was hard to pinpoint) it was removed on an outpatient basis! Today, I'm cancer-free and the buck stops here.

You Were There

By Wanda J. Burnside

Lord, You were there
When tears rolled down my face,
And when I fell again
In painful disgrace.

You were there
When my plans crumbled to my feet,
And when I walked away
In bitter defeat.

You were there
When my life was falling apart,
And when I didn't know
Where to go or where to start.

You were there
When there were lies, scandals and shame,
And when everyone somehow
Forgot my name.

You were there
When friends left me one by one,
And when I hopelessly thought
Nothing could be done.

You were there
When death took my loved ones away,
And when I felt like
I couldn't go on another day.

You were there
When the doctor's report was bad,
And when my heart was
Fearful, heavy, and sad.

You were there
In the morning before
The birds began to sing,
And in the midnight
When I worried about everything.

Lord, You were there
When I turned and ran back to You.
You lovingly held me
And gave me life anew!

Copyright 2002

I don't need to tell you that these are hard economic times, (but I will). In 2008, I nearly lost my home to foreclosure. Hopefully, the following testimony will help you.

Both before and after Rev. Edwards made his transition, I tried to sell my home. The first time a total of 30 people looked at the home, loved it, but no one placed a single bid. After Reverend passed, I put it back on the market. Three real estate people tried to sell it, including our son. Nothing happened. Finally, I asked the Lord, *"Why can't I sell this house?"* His response was a rebuke:

"Because you never asked me how I felt about your selling MY house and moving to Texas."

Holy fear and trembling came upon me. Of course, He was right. We had asked God to bless us to sell the house so that we could move to Texas. We prayed the wrong prayer. We didn't ask permission to move to Texas. Sure there is a mortgage meltdown. But my issue wasn't an economic one. It was one of disobedience. We are told to acknowledge God in all our ways and He will direct our paths. (Proverbs 3:5-6). Guess why I'm still here? Right!

After this rebuke from the Lord, I found myself falling on my face and entering into a new prayer zone. Immediately, I repented and turned over every worldly possession to the Lord. Feel free to ease drop on one of my conversations with Him:

"Father, please forgive me for my independent spirit. I did not acknowledge you in this situation. Indeed, the house I'm living in is YOUR house. Therefore, this is YOUR house note. I'm happy to be a doorkeeper in YOUR house. Thank you for your forgiveness."

At the time of this prayer, the mortgage on this house was seven months behind and I watched how God worked it all out. Now, I'm living in a mortgage-free home! TO GOD BE THE GLORY!

I heard the Lord saying, *"When I'm first in line, I will take care of what's mine."*

Now, here's another example of God's faithfulness...

A couple of years following my husband's death I went Christmas shopping. I didn't realize that I had overspent until I went to the ATM machine. That's when I discovered that I only had $3.29 in my bank account! And it would be two more weeks before I would have any more money. I was panic-stricken. That's when I heard the Voice of the Lord:

"Mary, didn't I give the children of Israel manna in the wilderness every day? (Exodus 16:50) Can't I give you bread (money) every day?"

Suddenly, my faith took a quantum leap and my response was, "*Yes, Lord, You can do anything.*"

Friends, from that day to this, I receive money every day. Sometimes a little. Sometimes a lot. But every day. For instance, one day after my home mail had come and there was nothing there but bills, I went to my ministry's post office box and there was nothing there either. I said to the Lord, "*Lord, the sun is nearly down and I haven't received any 'bread' all day.*" The words had barely been spoken, when I looked down at my feet and there was a dime! I shouted as though it was $1,000. Great is God's faithfulness.

Another time when God spoke clearly to me about receiving bread was when I was tossing out some stale bread. The Voice of the Lord said, "*Don't throw that bread away.*" "*But, Lord, it's stale.*"

"*Give it to the birds,*" was God's response. I did. It was a joy to watch the birds congregate immediately around the stale bread. In 15 minutes, the bread was completely devoured. And I put nearly a whole loaf out there! "*Just as you feed these birds, I will feed you,*" saith the Lord.

Friends, my vision for ministry and personal needs is so great that I've gone from asking God for crumbs, to a slice, to a loaf, to a BAKERY! He is going to give it to me because I have faith to believe. And I'm rolling in dough!

He is the Bread of Life (John 6:35). And there is enough for all of us!

By now you can see that I love to testify. Stay with me for one more personal testimony. I call it my Leaves of Gold testimony.

When my late husband was alive, I could afford a housekeeper and a gardener. Sadly, some things have changed.

The other day I looked out of the window and saw a mountain of leaves. *"Oh, no! Another job to do. Lord, send me some help."*

That's when the Lord spoke to me through the following poem.

Leaves of Gold

Please, Please, Please
Look at the leaves
As they fall from the trees
Heavens windows have opened up
God's blessings will fill your cup
Surely, you will sip and you will sup

Wealth is being spread around
Your bank account will abound,
Beloved, make a joyful sound

Jump, shout, praise his holy name
Your life will never be the same
My word you can claim

2 Chronicles 20:20
And they rose early in the morning, and went forth into the wilderness of Tekoa: and as they went forth, Jehoshaphat stood and said, Hear me, O Judah, and ye inhabitants of Jerusalem; Believe in the LORD your God, so shall ye be established; believe his prophets, so shall ye prosper.

After receiving this word from the Lord, I have a whole new perspective when I look at leaves. In fact, I want to keep every one of them! When I look at the various colors, I see that the brown ones represent old money; the green ones, new money, the gold ones, best money. I even saved a bag and kept it in my garage. Last winter I went out to gather some to give away to friends. They were cold. The Lord spoke again and said, *"Cold cash coming!"* I believe God. So do those friends whom I've given them to for a reminder.

If you received a bag of leaves from me and have a testimony, I'd like to hear it.

Email: edwardsmd@sbcglobal.net.

In November of 2008 after God inspired me with the leaves incident, I started my business and named it *"Leaves of Gold Consulting, LLC."*

I Can See Clearly Now
By Missionary Claudette Slappy

When I was asked to write about the most devastating thing that has ever happened to me, and how I dealt with it, I didn't have to think twice about what that experience was.

Although life has dealt me quite a few experiences to choose from, nothing has quite impacted me and affected my life as losing most of my vision and being told that I was going to be blind. I have been diagnosed with diabetic retinopathy: a disease caused by diabetes.

In 1983, I was told that I was a *"border-line"* diabetic and needed to begin to manage my diet and exercise. Unwisely, I ignored the diagnosis until 1991, at which point, I began to take my medication sporadically, whenever I thought about it. All along, the diabetes was silently doing its damage.

It was in 1998 that I found out that the diabetes had done significant damage to my eyes by causing the blood vessels behind them to burst. I was sent to several specialists and endured countless laser treatments to reduce the number of damaged vessels behind my eyes. This was to no avail. After these unsuccessful treatments, I had to have invasive surgery in both eyes, hoping to restore and repair the damage that had occurred. Thus far, the surgery has prevented complete blindness, but my vision has been significantly altered.

This upset in my life was quite devastating to me because I've always been an avid reader. I can remember, as a child, how I would go to the public library after school and would stay until it was almost dark. Looking back, I can even remember thinking that the worse thing in the world to happen to someone was to be blind. That became a reality for me in 2001 when I was told that my vision had degenerated and was now so bad that I was confirmed as *"legally blind."*

Upon being informed that I was now legally blind, I thought I would never be able to read again. For three months or so, I did nothing but cry and pray. I was waiting on God to heal me, but it didn't happen. I told the Lord that I couldn't wait on Him any longer and that I had to move on with my life. My declaration was exactly what God wanted me to do. He wanted me to take the first step and He would do the rest. If it had not been for my faith and trust in God, I know that I would not have been able to deal with my partial vision loss at all.

My recommendation to anyone going through whatever crisis it may be would be to trust the Lord. He's always there. Remember, nothing is impossible with God. Thanks to the Lord and medical technology, I am now able to drive (with limitations) and help with what is called a *"bioptic lens."* To God be the glory!

> *Claudette Sappy is the widow of Pastor James E. Slappy, Jr., founder of Calvary Church of God in Christ. She is a mother, grandmother, great grandmother, and ministers to many in Michigan and beyond.*

Hole in My Heart Filled by Grace
By Brenda McGee

Being born with a hole in my heart was just the beginning of my persistent struggle to maintain some normalcy in my life, while growing up in a family plagued with mental illness and discord. The extent of my condition manifested itself some years later, but my utmost concern was the growing instability of my family.

I first became aware that things were not quite right in my family when I was five years old. I had just returned from living a whole year away from home, which I found out had been an arrangement agreed upon by my parents. I also learned later that I was not the only child in my family who had been parceled off to live elsewhere. Strange as it may seem, people did this back then and thought nothing of it.

I suspected that my siblings and I had been separated and sent to live in various places because my parents were having trouble in their marriage. I was right. Mom, who married at age16, later revealed that my dad had indeed been unfaithful to her. My mother was a beautiful woman. This was hard to believe.

This was the start of my mother's mental illness, which would carry over into the next decade with countless trips in and out of psychiatric institutions in several states. Being heavily medicated during her stays in the hospital, Mom did not remember everything clearly, but I remember it all too well. I had to take up the slack (caring for my younger siblings, cooking my dad's meals, and doing other domestic chores) whenever my mother was away. Plus, I had to keep up with schoolwork -- not an easy task, but I managed somehow.

Between hospitalizations, I would pray that Mom's condition would stabilize. She would be okay for a month or two; then she would slip back into sleepless nights – sometimes weeks at a time, exhibiting embarrassing and obnoxious behaviors, getting violent and verbally abusive, or walking off somewhere and talking to complete strangers. Imagine what it was like at parent-teacher conferences.

Even when home, I had to watch Mom closely for signs of depression, which could lead to another episodic event. My father tended to only make matters worse with his abusive behavior and demeaning remarks. He would always criticize Mom about something. He had gotten so far away from godly principles that he had been taught as a child. My older brother suffered from mental illness too and a younger brother became profoundly retarded due to a childhood illness.

I sought God about all of these matters and what he revealed to me set me on a course that enabled me to conquer the demons in my family. He revealed that certain relatives were passive vessels in our family. In other words, they were not the aggressive type, but rather mild-mannered in nature. This is not necessarily bad, but the enemy took occasion to attack these weaker family members by getting control of their minds. The enemy used my father to attack them as well. Having already yielded himself to lustful temptations, Satan used him to help fulfill his evil deeds. When God enlightened me about this, I knew exactly how to pray.

Since then, God has taken care of the hole in my heart. It is still there, but it has never prevented me from living a successful and rewarding life. God continues to bless my family. My mother has not had a setback in years. Had it not been for my grandmother's instilling in me an explicit faith and trust in the Almighty at an early age, I shutter to think what my life could have been like without God's mercy and grace.

> *Brenda E. (Hampton) McGee was born in Brooklyn, New York. She is an author, educator, poet and playwright. Her inspirational and heartfelt writings stretch across the generations to reach people of all ages, backgrounds, and cultural origins with messages of love, courage, hope, and peace.*
>
> *Email: bhmcgee01@yahoo.com*

Married To A Mean Man

I fully understand why adultery is committed. I get why people take the easy way out of a marriage. It's so you can feel like more than a paycheck, or a new pair of shoes, or a new car. It's so you can feel like you have a purpose in life again. So you can know people DO like you and everything you do isn't wrong.

Yes, I have thought of taking a lover, just leaving and never looking back. I could do it. I could become the woman I used to be years ago. I could pull my OWN strings.

But would I really be that same woman who stood in the sanctuary so long ago? I was in a pretty dress, holding beautiful flowers, and very much in love. I almost shouted my vows.

You see, no one signs up to be pushed aside years later. No one agrees to be part of domestic abuse. And it is a form of abuse when your heart is neglected and your love thrown back at you. No one wants to be shown that even their spouse doesn't enjoy their company anymore. Who wants to only be touched during a church service in front of other people?

The rub is that we make these vows not only to man but God also. We forget that in the silence of not being spoken to and the vastness of being the only one in your once *"marriage bed."* But we did promise God to hang in there no matter what.

One day, in the grocery store, my husband had just walked off refusing to answer me and I said aloud, *"Lord, deliver me from an inconsiderate man!"* A woman next to me asked if he fought me, drank or gambled. I said, *"No."* She asked if he brought his money home. I said, *"It comes in the mail."* She asked if he had a gun to my head. I said. *"No."* She concluded her inquiry with these words, *"Then, you're ahead of the game."* I looked at my cart and smiled. But when I looked up she was gone, nowhere in sight in any aisle. Scripture tells us, *"Be not forgetful to entertain strangers: for thereby some have entertained angels unawares"* (Hebrews 13:2). I think she was my angel answering my cry for help.

Keeping my faith intact and my vow to God truly is my goal. When there's silence, it means nothing mean is being said. I know once again that I have worth and purpose and I know I have kept my covenant with God. Mr. Mean has not and cannot make me break my promise to God. That is more important to me than anything or anyone.

So, divorce is not an option for me; nor is adultery. I just have to bite the bullet knowing that in my Father's house there are many mansions and one with my name on it ------- unless it gets physical.

~ *by The Wife of a Mean Man*

Five Year Turn Around
By Minister Dessie Morgan

This morning I am reflecting on my life as a married woman and now as a widow. Our God is awesome! He is faithful, and His word is undisputed. His compassion and love are unending. In this season of transition, I can only say, *"Thank You, Lord."*

My testimony is to the glory of God and that He will reward them who are diligently seeking Him. He will meet every need, according to His riches in glory by Christ Jesus. This is not a cliché. This is life experienced firsthand.

I want to reach women who were unprepared when death knocked at the door of their love one. I was one of them that did not want to deal with the issue of death. Rather than prepare, I avoided it until it was too late. The knock came. Fred and I were not prepared financially. Many widows are left in this state of destitution.

My husband was diagnosed in October 2000 with cancer. He was given one year to live but my God gave him four years more. Fred and I prayed, and we made a decision to trust God to meet my needs should he pass. We committed to live to the fullest and not worry.

My home, which is though a ministry, is to train men with special needs to live independently in the community. Fred and I were the first husband and wife team in this ministry. One month after Fred's death, the guys graduated and moved into their apartment. At that time, the ministry made the decision not to continue the program and to close the home.

But God, being the God that He is, remembered my faithfulness to His word and my husband. He led me to Isaiah 54:5, *"For thy maker is thine husband; the Lord of Hosts is his name; and thy Redeemer the Holy One of Israel; the God of the whole earth shall he be called."* That day He became my husband. I say this to every widow, Allow God to replace that void that was left empty by your mate and allow Him to become your husband.

My home was scheduled to close in October 2005. I cried out to God for His desire for me in this season. My supervisor came by to tell me the news of the closing but, as she was telling me this, there was a rumbling going on in my spirit. When she left, I sought God, and worshiped Him. He heard my cry and met my every need.

The Lord directed me to write a letter to our board of directors, and I shared it with our founder of the ministry. She read the letter and said, *"Dessie, this is everything I wanted to say. This is straight from the heart of God."* That letter was sent to all the board members. The contents of that letter allowed those doors to remain open. In my heart, I knew that God would not allow my earthly husband to be with Him and I become homeless.

Seven days after my letter went out I checked my emails and saw one from my supervisor that said *"Miracle."* My heart was pounding and I knew, at that time, God heard my husband's prayer and on that day God moved on my behalf. I opened the email and read that an anonymous donor gave $500,000 dollars over a five-year period for our home. On that day I regained strength and began seeing life anew knowing that God heard my husband's prayer for me!

We are now into the fifth year of Fred's death and God has been true to his Word. God's Word to me was that he was going to do something for me in that five-year span. He spoke in a still small voice that, *"You have been faithful to another man's vision and now I can trust you with My vision."*

The Lord began to deal with me regarding the men that I have been given stewardship over. The area of distress for them is maintaining employment. I have fought many battles fighting for their jobs. One morning in prayer I receive the word from the Lord to train and employ them. He said that He had given me the passion and the formula to train them.

The formula is to 1. Tell them. 2. Show them. 3. Let them. 4. Correct them. 5. Repetition, Repetition, Repetition, Success!

The Lord gave me the vision three years ago for a portable deli that can be setup on site at different churches and we would start with my church in Detroit and the guy's church in Livonia. I went to my pastor and shared the vision. He embraced it and said, *"Let's do it."* I then went to the guy's church and the pastor took it before their board. The support was outstanding. The church put together a Special Need Worship Service where the guys were part of the worship team. They ushered, served communion with the pastor, read Scripture, and ministered to the people with the pastor. The sense of pride and their self-esteem went to another level.

I begin to seek the heart of the Lord regarding the vision and a place to train the guys. I knew It was a conflict of interest to do this in our home, as tempting as it was. Anxiousness began to take over. I had to stop and worship the Lord where true release and victory has always been successful for me.

I began to drive and look at office buildings, looked at closed restaurants, searched Craig's List, all the time trusting God. I looked at our family restaurant, but that did not work out. I finally found a place that could be converted and called Ms. Fay, one of my guy's (Brian) mother, and she has embraced this vision. I did not see the excitement in her eyes, but I knew this was it. I called the executive director of our ministry. She went to observe. Although she had a dubious look on her face, she tried not to interfere with my faith. I called up my children, and there was not a positive connection there. They did not want me to get into a lease I could not get out of.

In my excitement, I requested my vacation money early so I could put down the deposit. I went to pick up the check and I heard a still small voice in my spirit that said, *"Don't do it."* I prayed that entire weekend asking the Lord for clarity. Guess what? No answer. So I held onto the monies.

That Monday morning my friend and spiritual daughter called me and asked, *"Did you put the money on that place?"* I told her I hadn't. She said, *"Call my sister. There is a new place opening in Detroit for entrepreneurs and they have openings for restaurants."* I felt a leap in my spirit, like this could be it. I called the number. The young lady answered and told me to come on down. I went there and the rest is history. I am now a restaurant owner certified by the City of Detroit, The guys are now employees of the restaurant. Their families are involved in helping us build our business by investing in their training.

At this moment, I am in the midst of that five-year turnaround, which is October 28, 2009. Fred and I were married on October 28. To add to that, our kick off in the guy's church was on Fred's birthday, June 7, 2009. I believe the prayers that Fred prayed for me are still being answered. God is honoring my natural marriage, and the completion of that era, by confirming Himself as my Spiritual Husband. This is what He said when Fred departed this life on earth.

Now I hear the Lord saying *"Expansion."* I don't know how this will happen, but my faith tells me that it is done. I agree with His Word, and I know that this will take place by October, which is the completion of the five years.

Minister Dessie Morgan is an ordained minister, author, entrepreneur, home coordinator and trainer for 17 men teaching them to live independently in the community. She is a widow, mother and grandmother. She enjoys traveling and has been to many countries, including the Holy Land, China, Paris and Germany.

The Miracle Man

By Francisco (Frank) Garcia

Anyone who doesn't believe in miracles needs to hear my story. I've been challenged by sickness, illness, and have even been at the doors of death. Only my faith in the Creator has allowed me to survive.

To begin with, I was conceived 10 years after doctors told my parents they would never have anymore children. They already had lost twin boys shortly after birth and had two other still-born babies. I have been called a *"Miracle Baby."* God always has the last word. Three brothers and twin sisters followed my birth. We all are miracle babies.

Miracle number two happened when I was seven. My dad and I were building a crystal radio set and I was struck by lightning. The lightning increased all of my sensory perceptions to inhuman levels. I had to attend the medical facilities at Wayne State University in Detroit to be tested every year until I turned 21.

Miracle number three occurred when my wife Claudette and I decided to do some early morning shopping. As we pulled up to a stop sign, a van ran the stop sign and collided head on with us. We didn't get a scratch, but our vehicle was totaled.

In March 1990, I fell 32 feet and shattered my left knee, causing many painful operations throughout the years. The doctors proclaimed that I would never walk again. Ha! Since then I've not only walked but JOGGED! You can't tell me that wasn't a miracle.

In 2000, I was diagnosed with congestive heart failure. The next year I received a pacemaker. The pacemaker went haywire over and over again and I ended up in the emergency ward of many hospitals because of the lost of electrolytes. The last time I went I was near death, and I do believe that my spirit left my body and came back. I recall praying, *"Lord, I don't want to keep living like this, but I don't want to die."* Later, I discovered that my wife, Claudette, who was still in the waiting room, was aware of that happening and begged God not to let me die. He answered both of our prayers and extended my life.

Because of my various health issues, the medical community had given me up for dead. However, I refused to accept their prognosis. I knew that God would let me know when my time was up, and it wasn't. Shortly after my near-death experience in the hospital's emergency room, I was sent to the University of Michigan Hospital. Three days later I received a brand new heart. That was in February 2006 and I haven't had any heart trouble since then. My new heart came from a 30-year-old donor. And I feel as though the Lord has renewed my youth like the eagle described in Psalm 103:5.

Of course, like all of God's people, I still have challenges. In March of this year, I was in another auto accident. The car was totaled, but I walked away without a single scratch.

Indeed, I've been tested. But I never gave up my faith in God or myself. Faith is one of God's greatest blessings, without which I wouldn't be here to relate these stories. May God bless you, one and all, and never lose your faith.

Francisco (Frank) Garcia started his professional career as a vocalist/violinist at the age of three. He has had recording contracts with ABC Paramount and Motown Records. He has performed with many great artists such as The Spinners, The Miracles, Stevie Wonder, and Lou Rawls. Frank and his wife, Claudette, are the founders of The Original Historical Music Society of Detroit and Astro Chemistry Records and Filmworks.

My Maker Is My Husband

By Tina Banks

My greatest challenge in life was when I became divorced. It was a big step for me physically, emotionally, and mentally. But, even more so, spiritually. I had been with my husband for 10 years. Since I was 18.

How do you become a single parent at the age of 28, with three children ages 10, 5 and six months old? My whole world was turned upside down and inside out. Over and over again, I wondered, *"How will we make it?"* I had no job.

What troubled me the most was the questioning look on my children's faces saying *"What's wrong mommy?"* Their little world and their home was being torn apart.

Although I didn't have a clue as to what to do, I knew that I had to be strong for my children and to make the transition as smooth as possible.

Because I lacked spiritual maturity at the time, I tried to take matters into my own hands. My poor decisions engulfed me like a roaring tornado tripping through a city. I knew I needed someone wiser than myself to take control of my life. At this point, I turned to God.

The closer I got to God and my church family, things began to calm down from the whirlwind tornado in our lives. One Scripture that leaped out with my name on it was, *"I'll never leave you nor forsake you"* (Hebrews 13:5). I believed God. What a difference a word from God will make.

Once I refocused on who He is and whose I am, in time and with patience, I learned that God can handle any and everything. He created this entire universe. Surely, He can take care of my children and me.

In fact, He said He would be a father to the fatherless, (Psalm 68:5), and my Maker is my Husband, (Isaiah 54:5).

> *Tina Banks is the mother of four children. She attends Wings of Love Missionary Baptist Church in Detroit and has a passion for volunteering to help women and children in domestic violence centers.*
>
> *Email: isis514@sbcglobal.net*

God's Instrument of Hope
By Beverly Miller

During my younger years, I was always very healthy and athletic. But, as I got older, I started to develop lots of medical problems. When I reached my mid-forties, I was hit by one of my biggest challenges of all.

Part Three

In July of 1993, I was in the shower when I felt something in my breast. It was sore and thick. Because I had experienced cysts in my younger years, I just figured it was something like that. But this time it was sore and it was not round. It felt strange.

My mother died in 1989 from breast cancer. Since there was a family history, I started doing breast self exams every month. I had what is now called *"fibrocystic breast."* I say that I was *"tumor-prone."*

Not wanting to waste any time, I went to see my doctor immediately. He said, *"Beverly this is out of my league. I am going to send you to a breast specialist."* I went to see the specialist and he said I needed to take another mammogram. I had just had one in February, which came back normal.

When the results came back, I was told that I needed to have a lumpectomy for a biopsy to see if it were cancerous. Well, it was cancer. I was devastated at the news. Just thinking about my mother dying from the same disease caused me many tears and much worry about my own future. I prayed very hard and promised God that if He would heal me I would help others to conquer this horrible disease.

During my many talks with God, He took my faith to a whole new level. I learned that if we just keep believing in Him, He will strengthen us and turn our mustard seed faith into mountain moving faith. If we just let go and let God work in our lives, the Great Physician will heal us: spirit, soul and body..

After having between 25-30 surgeries, I still keep my faith, On July 21, 2009, I will be a 16-year breast cancer survivor. I kept my promise to God and I have been able to help many people with the work that I do. I consider myself God's instrument of hope.

> *Mrs. Beverly J. Miller lives in Michigan and volunteers with different cancer foundations. She brings hope through sharing her testimony of healing on television, radio, and in the newspapers.*
> *Email: miller3677@sbcglobal.net*

Turn In Your Badge
By Ramelle T. Lee

The workday started as usual with interface with my employees and overseeing their work assignments. I looked forward to continuing to supervise a busy staff at our state-of-the-art healthcare facility. However, things suddenly changed directions. I was sitting in my office adjacent to the director's office, when I received a phone call. "Ramelle, can I see you in my office for a few minutes?" It was my boss. I didn't hesitate to respond to her request. Immediately, I walked across the hall and entered the doorway. Upon walking in, I was taken aback when I noticed the Human Resources Representative was sitting there. This was a complete surprise to me.

My life, that afternoon at 2:30p.m on January 14, 2002, instantly changed. Was I prepared for what was getting ready to happen? Yes and no, let me explain.

Our department employees were notified months ago that we would be down sizing. Eight of our employees would lose their job, due to economic motivated reductions in the workforce. Throughout the hospital system, hundreds of workers were going through the same process and hearing the same speech. It was my turn to receive the news.

God doesn't make mistakes. I listened to the explanation of why I was losing my job after 31 years of employment. Strangely, I received the news well and very calmly accepted the outcome. Many signs were already there in weeks past. Job functions were being streamlined, reorganized or eliminated throughout our department and the hospital system.

When you are placed in a situation that you have no control over, it takes your faith to see you through the tough times. God prepared me months ago to handle this dramatic and abrupt change. I didn't understand what was about to happen to me, but God wanted me to change my mindset and get my finances in order.

Back in November of 2001, during my devotion time, I was puzzled when I asked the Lord, what I should read that morning and He spoke the name, "Naaman" in my spirit. So I immediately checked the Bible concordance and located 2 Kings 5 and read the entire chapter. The Lord's message to me was this...

"My child, you need to receive a healing of your finances. It's time that you look seriously at this situation and know that the Holy Spirit is here to guide and direct you. Your finances are in a leprosy state.

Just like Naaman was not willing to do as my prophet had instructed him, you have not been willing to do as I have instructed. It's time that you pay attention to the leading of the Holy Spirit. You need to get out of debt. You are on the right track when it comes to seeding, but you still have not stopped spending. You are not disciplined in this area. Take those credit cards and put them away. Do not charge any more items until you get yourself a plan as to how you are going to clean up the balances on your accounts. Start with the small balances first and work your way up to the large balances."

I put the credit cards up! That same evening, when I came home from work, I had a letter from Breakthrough Ministries with Pastor Rod Parsley. The ministry letter that I received was about Naaman from 2 Kings 5:1.

"Now Naaman, captain of the host of the King of Syria...a mighty man of valour, but he was a leper" **(2 Kings 5:1)**

As I continued to read the letter from Breakthrough Ministries, I knew that was confirmation that I had to turn my financial situation around. Naaman wanted the prophet Elisha to speak a word of healing because he was a powerful man. He couldn't understand why he was being requested to go down to the River of Jordan and dip seven times.

Part Three

"Then went he down, and dipped himself seven times in Jordan, according to the saying of the man of God: and his flesh came again like unto the flesh of a little child, and he was clean"
(2 Kings 5:14).

Naaman received his miraculous healing. I knew that God wanted me to believe for a financial miracle breakthrough. I released my faith and embraced the scripture in this message which referred me to Isaiah 41:10. In every area of my life, God says, *"Fear Thou Not."* Through faith, I obeyed the word of the Lord and sowed a special offering seed of $41.10 believing God to set me free from the spirit of fear dealing with my finances being in a leprosy state.

God showed me how to trust Him and believe that He would turn my situation around. I immediately followed my financial plan and began to pay down my credit cards. Through my severance pay received from my former employer, I began to eliminate the debt.

When you walk with God, He will work everything out for your good. It's clear that if I had not listened to the *"Voice of the Lord"* regarding my finances, that I would not have handled being released from my job shortly afterwards in a calm way. God already knew what was about to happen and He was preparing me for this abrupt change. The Holy Ghost already knew exactly what I would do. Are you listening to His small still voice?

Getting back to the part about me losing my job. I now work for God, as a Christian author and poet.

Since then, I've published my first book entitled, "*Step Into His Greatness*." This book of prophetic meditation messages of the Lord encourages us to walk worthy of our calling in Christ Jesus.

Like Naaman, I received my healing in more ways than one. God is still perfecting those things that concern me.

> *Ramelle Lee resides in Detroit, Michigan. She is a long time member of Greater Bethlehem Missionary Baptist Church. She is devoted to her mother, Barbara Lee, and her twin brother Rev. Lovell Lee. Lee's work is well received all over the world.*
>
> *She can be reached at ramelleskip@aol.com or www.thecalledandreadywriters.org.*

Survivor

By Dr. DeBorah Donald

"But unto you that fear my name shall the Sun of righteousness arise with healing in his wings; and ye shall go forth, and grow up as calves of the stall" (Malachi 4:2)

Looking back over my life, I can clearly see that God is with me. It is like an outer body experience, or being carried up to a high mountain on the wings of an angel and looking down on your life. It's like getting a new pair of glasses. When properly fitted, they will allow you to see well.

It was a cold dreary day, at about 12:45 p.m., on November 3, 2003, when my horrible journey began. I was sitting in my office chair talking with a colleague when the room began to go in and out. My right eye ached as if it had been punched with a brick. A tear-like fluid ran down my face. My tongue was frozen and swollen on one side. My speech was slurred. And my right arm was tingling and going numb at the same time. Trying to talk, I began to rebuke the stroke demon that was attacking me.

Once at the hospital, a sense of comfort came over me. Now I could prove that what had attacked me was now gone. The hospital staff performed tests to rule out a stroke. The tests revealed that I did, in fact, have a full stroke and two small ones. While looking for blood on my brain, a large tumor was discovered. From that point, everything spiraled downward.

When I was diagnosed with these life-threatening illnesses, I was in the prime of my life. I was going places. Every day was the best day of my life and I celebrated it by giving God thanks throughout the day. I considered myself a committed Christian. I paid my tithes and offerings, went to church regularly, prayed for all my adversaries, known and unknown. I was active on all levels of my denomination, and even sat on two major community boards. I am a pastor's wife and a marriage and layman counselor and teacher. Within a few seconds, my life no longer resembled itself. The tables had turned and, at that point, I became the one in need of a counselor. I had been told that if a surgeon would agree to perform the operation needed to survive, there would only be a 20-25% chance of some continued *"normal life."*

Suddenly the need to praise God with all that is within me became first. The words of the Lord became real and leaped off the pages of the Bible into my spirit and began to encourage my soul. Life is a conflict with survival. We are the righteousness of God, and there is strength down on the inside that springs up when we need it to allow the effectiveness of God to take full control of our lives. Illness is just another obstacle that will be moved through faith. Belief in God's Word is the best medicine. It supersedes anything else that man has to offer. God has an investment in me that is a treasure that activates itself when needed!

Initially, I could not see my healing; I did not feel delivered because I was in pain. But when I cried out to the Lord, He recognized my cry. When I could not pray for myself, my cry lifted me. My stored up praises took over, and when the pain pill did not work, when the time for the pain shot was an hour away, the Lord released an assurance that had been shut up in my heart that went all through my body with every heartbeat. He broke the pain in my flesh. Suddenly I had more vision than anything. I could see myself healed!

Determined to beat all or any odds, at night I practiced how to smile, lick out my tongue, wink my right eye and strengthen my right side. Image that. These bodily functions that I took so for granted were now mountains to be conquered.

My family fights this brain tumor battle with me. I am a survivor! The spirit of bondage has been lifted. Now I have a business, conduct sessions of encouragement, go to churches and give my testimony. God brought me out of the darkness of no hope. He reminded me that healing is in His wings and that Jesus was whipped so that I could be delivered. With every stripe I am healed in the precious name of Jesus.

Some say it is a blessing to be called a survivor. More importantly, is the fact that you remain a survivor. I never dreamed that I would be a stroke/brain tumor survivor. However, now I truly believe there is a balm in Gilead and it is for me!

"Is there no balm in Gilead; is there no
physician there? why then is not the health
of the daughter of my people recovered?
(Jeremiah 8:22).

De`Borah A. Donald, Ph.D. was born in Detroit, MI. She is a pastor's wife, public relations chairperson to S.W. # 1 Jurisdiction C.O.G.I.C., licensed evangelist, an educator, and a First Responder Lieutenant Certified Chaplain. Her writings are real-life experiences that encourage all people with messages that God is love and all that we need is in Him.

Faith: Use it or Lose It!

He Sustains Me

By Emma Avery

"Cast your cares on the Lord and he will sustain you" (Psalm 55:22a).

The song says, *"Through many dangers, toils, and snares I have already come."* I am told that I was a breech born baby at birth in 1947, but I survived. Then, five months after my birth, a cousin felt that I didn't deserve to live, so she decided to take it into her own hands and try to end my life. She picked me up in her arms and spoon-fed me some lye. I was snatched from the jaws of death again. Later on in my life, I was plagued with pneumonia. Not once, but three times - in both of my tiny fragile lungs. But death was not on my agenda... and I lived again.

Some may say, *"That is enough, and she can't handle anything else."* Not true. Along comes the front porch swing and my sister.

As I sat in the swing on a beautiful summer day, my sister decided to take a run across the long porch and take an acrobatic jump into the swing beside me. As she did, down came the swing, which was being supported with a broken rusty nail that plunged into the top of my head. My screams were agonizing and Grandma rushed to my aid and found the rusty nail stuck in my head. After pulling it out, she closed the hole in my head with old cobwebs! Only God knows why I survived that without any crippling consequences.

If that weren't enough to contend with at such an early age, there were some dirty older men who took it upon themselves to thrust more pain upon me and sexually abused me. Then they played up to my grandparents as if they weren't doing anything wrong to me

My life moved forward and I thought things were getting better and I was on my way to becoming a world-class athlete, but my whole world came to a screeching standstill.

In 1963, I had just celebrated my Sweet Sixteenth birthday and started attending high school. Shortly afterwards, I was named Outstanding Athlete of the Year. How cool was that? Not cool at all. Three months later I woke up in a hospital room strapped to the bed as excruciating pain surged through my body in the worse kind of way. The first words I heard were, *"Peace. Be Still."* Looking around to see who was there with me, (for I really don't see anyone) I heard it again and this time the voice seemed a bit sweeter as if it were wrapping itself around me. I was confused about where I was; however, I was not afraid, the voice had brought a total calm around me. I soon learned that both of my legs had been amputated in a terrible train and car accident that took the life of my aunt. I had to learn a lot of things again and the hardest one of all was learning to walk

It was a long time before I shared with anyone about the calming voice I heard that horrible day.

When I did, I got the reaction that I felt I would get. People looked at me as if I had lost my mind. That voice I have come to know is the voice of JESUS. That voice has always been my guide through so much pain, abuse and misunderstanding. Whenever things seem to be getting the best of me, Jesus always comes to me saying, *"Peace. Be still."* He knew what I didn't know that He was carrying me and I really didn't have to worry. That voice is still speaking into my mind and heart. Because of that, my life is not as complicated as others may see it.

After recovering from such a devastating thing, sadness once again found its way back into my life. My mom and I traveled back South where the accident happened to take care of some business and my life was invaded by another sexual abuse by someone claiming to be there to help.

After many surgeries, I had to face another painful and scary surgery. In 2004, I was told that I would have to have my left hip joint replaced if I wanted to lead a normal and less painful life.

Praise the Lord. I can say that all went well with that surgery, and I am walking again. Not as much, or as pain free as in the past, but thanks to my Lord and Savior, I am walking.

Since my hip surgery, I've been diagnosed with a pinched nerve in my lower back, which is extremely painful. But I praise God that I am still able to do as much as I can and doing well within my spirit. That is what keeps me going.

If I had given up... if I had quit... if God had not been there within my soul... if the Lord had not wrapped His arms around me and covered my life with His blood, I am not sure where I would be, nor what type of lifestyle I would be living now. Who knows? I might have become a drug addict, because of the pain, a prostitute, because of the sexual abuse, or even a fatality.

I said it before and I will say it again, *"Through many dangers, toils, and snares I have already come."* And I am here to confess that my faith in GOD, and His son JESUS, whom I have accepted as my Lord and Savior, is still strong. I have no reason to fear man and mean deeds. I know I will survive and everything will always be just fine. I have no need to worry. I am a *"kept"* woman and the Lord sustains me. THANK GOD for HIS LOVE.

In 1963, Emma was named athlete of the year at her high school. Shortly afterwards, she was involved in a deadly train and automobile accident, which left her a bilateral double leg amputee.

After many surgeries, she learned to use both prostheses well enough to walk without any type of aid and operates an automobile without hand controls. Having worked as a counselor, she motivates others with disabilities; has been affiliated with the Toastmasters; has shared on television, in newspapers, and hosted a radio talk show. Her first book will be published in September 2009. Emma lives a very rewarding and independent life.

Email: sunshynesplace@yahoo.com

Just before I bring this book to a close, I want to share with you the following testimony. It's written by a young man whom I haven't had the pleasure of meeting. After reading his story, there was absolutely no doubt in my mind that God wanted this project to go forth. Let me tell you why.

While writing the book, I had a section called *"Faith vs. Hope."* I had a very difficult time explaining the difference between the two because they are so closely associated. So I left that part out of the book. I'm still not sure that I can give a good enough definition of the difference. But when I got this testimony, I knew that God wanted us to meditate on these two words. I encourage you to do so. (That's your homework assignment!)

You Can't Have Hope Without Faith

By Dwayne Merritt

In 1991, Mother Lillian Sims gave her 10-year-old granddaughter Angel a word from God that has helped us keep our faith in our darkest hour 15 years later. Mother Sims told Angel she was going to have twins.

Being a 10-year-old little girl, Angel did not think anything of it. It was always a family joke throughout the years that Angel was going to have twins because *"Grandma said it."*

In 1986, at the age of six years old, I asked my mother when would I get married. After realizing that I was really serious, my mother prayed about it and told me that God said He has a wife hand picked for you and she is an *"Angel of a woman."* I held on to that word and in 1996 I met Angel Sims. At that time, Angel was 14 years old and I was 15 years old. I remember the word that my mother gave me but I had no idea that God would send me an angel named *"Angel."*

Angel and I remained high school sweethearts and we both accepted Jesus Christ as our Lord and Savior in 2001. We both were active members in our church and served on several auxiliaries. In 2006, Angel Sims became Angel Merritt and the first prophecy came to pass. Little did we know that the prophesy of Mother Sims was soon to follow.

After six months of being married, on a Sunday morning, one of the mothers of the church told Angel that she had a dream the night before and God told her that she was pregnant. Angel's response was, *"If I am pregnant, it is nothing but God."* Angel was on birth control and was not trying to get pregnant.

Immediately following Sunday morning service, another mother of the church approached Angel and said God told her that she was about to give birth. After the second confirmation, Angel left church and took a pregnancy test. After taking three tests, Angel came to grips that yes she was pregnant.

Angel became ill about a week after she found out she was pregnant. Her cousin took her to the emergency room because she thought she had the flu. I met them at the hospital and her cousin and I joked that she was probably sick because she is having twins like *"Grandma said."* After several test, and an ultrasound, the doctor came out and told me that we were having twins.

It was a difficult pregnancy and Angel was placed on bed rest very early in her pregnancy. After being off work for two months, she was feeling a little better and returned.

At 27 weeks pregnant, she got really ill at work and I had to pick her up. We were on our way home and Angel said, *"Something just doesn't feel right. Take me to the doctor."* Once there, we found out that she was in pre-term labor. The doctor immediately rushed us to the hospital and told us that he was concerned about baby A's heart. We were crushed.

After Angel was stabilized, we were sent to the cardiologist at the Children's Hospital of Michigan to have Baby A's heart checked. After the cardiologist checked the hearts of both babies, he said he also found a problem with Baby B's heart. He explained that he had not ever seen anything like this with a twin pregnancy. Both babies had two different heart issues. Baby A was diagnosed with Supraventricular Tachycardia. Her heart rate was 230 bpm, while a normal rate for a fetus should never exceed 160 bpm. It was diagnosed that Baby B's upper right heart valve was leaking into the lower chamber of the heart. Both babies' hearts were enlarged due to having to work extra hard to pump blood. The doctor stated if he gave Angel medication for one baby it would affect the other baby. So there was nothing that he could do.

I was at a crossroad in my faith. I asked myself, *"Should I believe God to be a Healer, or accept the doctor's report?"* After shedding a few tears, we decided to place our trust in God. On that day, we made a quality decision. While driving home from the hospital, I looked at my wife and told her to dry her tears because I believed the word that was spoken 15 years prior had to come to pass. We drove to the local furniture store and purchased two cribs for our baby girls, because we believe that faith without works is dead.

On October 6, 2007, two miracle baby girls were born named Hope and Faith, because without Faith there is no Hope. This was the toughest trial I have ever been faced with, because the faith that I preach had to rescue my daughters from death. God showed us that if we couldn't trust Him with our babies, He wouldn't trust us with His babies.

Elder Dwayne C. Merritt was born in Detroit, Michigan. After graduating from high school, he fell into a lifestyle of running the streets chasing after a false sense of worth. In February of 2000 he found himself sitting in a police station facing 30 years for a crime he did not commit. It was by the grace of God that the charges were dropped. Elder Merritt decided at that point that he would not take another step without first getting God's permission. He has been being led by the Lord ever since that day. He and his family attend El-Beth-El Temple in Detroit.

CONCLUSION

"Therefore, seeing we also are compassed about by so great a cloud of witnesses, let us lay aside every weight, and the sin which doth so easily beset us, and let us run with patience the race that is set before us" (Hebrews 12:2).

Hopefully, by now you have received an increase in your faith, as I have from writing this text and reading the testimonies. Please let me hear from you.

With regard to Hebrews 12:2, I am not a theologian and won't expound on this particular verse except to say, I don't know who *"so great a cloud of great witnesses"* may be who are watching us, but one thing I'm sure of is this: God is watching and I want Him to see me doing what He told me to do.

Father, I hope You are pleased. For this one thing I know…

WITHOUT FAITH IT IS IMPOSSIBLE TO PLEASE GOD
(Hebrews 11:6)

Finally, some of you may have received my Monday Morning Meditations throughout 2008. On May 19th, I sent out one called, *"Your Faith Will Get You There."* Little did I know then that I would be writing this book. Let me conclude with these words from the song, **"We've Come This Far My Faith."**

> *Chorus*
> *We've come this far by faith*
> *Leaning on the Lord*
> *Trusting in His Holy word*
> *He never failed me yet*
> *Oh' Can't Turn Around*
> *We've come this far by faith*   *(Repeat)*

<u>*Verse*</u>
Just the other day, I heard a man say
He did not believe in God's word
But I can truly say, the Lord has made a way
He's never failed me yet   *(Chorus)*

Oh, Can't Turn Around
We've come this far by faith

KEEP GOING SAINTS.
DON'T STOP NOW!

About the Author

In 2007, Minister Mary Edwards wrote her autobiography, <u>Born Grown</u>. She shares with the reader how, at the age of 13, she became a mother the same day she lost her virginity.

The school was horrified. Edwards was an honor roll student when this happened. The school predicted that now she would become just another negative welfare statistic. But God had a different plan.

At the age of 33, Edwards accepted Jesus Christ into her life. He changed man's doomsday prophecy for her into His divine destiny. Indeed, she has been on many rolls, but not the welfare rolls. Instead, she has received recognition from her city, county, governor, and even the President of The United States for her community work, including that of establishing programs to get mothers off the welfare rolls.

If you ask Edwards how she defied the odds, she will tell you that the day she heard the indictment against her she said within herself, "No. I'm better than that." At that point, she began to write the script for her life, not the way it was, but the way she wanted it to be. She gives God all the glory! She truly knows that without Him she can do nothing.

She is the co-founder of Joy of Jesus Ministries in Detroit; founder of Widows With Wisdom and The Called and Ready Writers.

Minister Mary Edwards resides in Detroit and attends Salvation Temple church. She is a mother, grandmother, great grandmother and the widow of the esteemed Reverend Eddie K. Edwards.

Other Books
By Minister Mary Edwards

- MORNING PAPERS (Devotional)
- THE FISH MARKET (Evangelism)
- HIS HEARTBEAT (Devotional)
- AT HIS FEET (Parables)
- PONDERINGS FROM THE HEART OF MARY (Parables)
- BORN GROWN (Autobiography)
- TRANSITION: FROM WIDOWHOOD TO WOMANOOD (How-To)

ORDER FORM

FAITH: Use It Or Lose It

(NOTE: Prices listed below include 6% sales tax + S/H)

QTY	Description	Price	Total
	Faith Book	**15.75**	
	TOTAL ENCLOSED:		

Discounts available on 10 copies or more.
Call for more information: (313) 341-4487

Name: _____

Phone: _____

Address: _____

City: _____State: _____ Zip: _____

Email: _____

Checks should be made payable to and Mail to:
Minister Mary Edwards
P.O. Box 21818 - Detroit, MI 48221
or go to
LeavesOfGoldConsulting.com
to place your order online.

www.ingramcontent.com/pod-product-compliance
Lightning Source LLC
LaVergne TN
LVHW021505080426
835509LV00018B/2408